The Diary of Charles Macneill, Farmer, 1892–1896

with a commentary by
L.M. Montgomery

Rock's Mills Press

PUBLISHED BY
Rock's Mills Press

For information, visit us online at www.rocksmillspress.com or email us at customer.service@rocksmillspress.com.

CONTENTS

Preface

In L.M. Montgomery's diary of 1925, she understakes the extraordinary and unexpected act of copying another diary, itself composed between 1892 and 1898, into her own handwritten account.

In an entry of August 4, 1923, Montgomery records that during a visit to PEI, her friend and cousin Alec Macneill presented her with his father Charles's old diary.

But, as always, the pleasantest hours of all were when the day was ended and the boys off to bed. Then May and Alec and I would get into the dining room and sit for a couple of hours around a lavish supper table—May is certainly a queen cook!—and eat and talk and laugh. Oh, laugh! It was delightful to be free to laugh with boon companions again. One evening in especial we laughed until we could laugh no more.

Alec produced a "diary" his father had kept for several years and we read it together. I don't think I ever read anything quite so delicious in my life. Charles Macneill was an odd sort of a man, whom as a child I always loved because he was so kind to children. But I think that both as a neighbor and a father he left a good deal to be desired. He inherited from his mother—his father was not one of "our" Macneills but his mother was—a queer streak of the Macneill literary knack—a tiny thread of gold running through the slag of a very commonplace character. It flashed out here and there in the diary in several naive, satiric entries which were so artless and spontaneous that I could actually hear old Charles Macneill uttering them. We laughed until the tears poured from our eyes.

Apart from the unconscious humor of the diary it gave me the keen, sad delight of a vanished world re-created. It made old Cavendish live again—the Cavendish of my childhood and girlhood. It was all there in those little shabby notebooks as no deliberate attempt at description could ever produce it. Men and women long dead lived there again as in yesterday. The little affairs of church and state in a remote P.E. Island farming community were reflected there as in a mirror. I looked in it and saw the world of my teens pass before my eyes again. Oh, yes, we laughed—but behind the laughter was a sigh—and that is the difference between the laughter of youth and the laughter of middle age.

Two years later, in March 1925, at a time when Montgomery describes herself as suffering from extreme anxiety (her husband, a Presbyterian minister, was subject to bouts of mentall illness), she copies the diary into her own handwritten journal. It is a big job, taking up 100 handwritten pages:

> I have finished the old diary. It has taken me several Sunday afternoons and meanwhile I have been writing my journal entries separately and will copy them down later. To any other person in the world Charles Macneill's old diary would be tedious to read and unthinkably tedious to copy. But to me every moment I spent in copying it was a delight. I was back again in a world where happiness reigned and problems were non-existent—for me at least. I was so much at his home when a child and young girl that every word he wrote brought back vividly some sweet memory of those past days and childish frolics and delights. The most commonplace statement seemed like a finger touching the keys of an organ and evoking melodies of haunting sweetness—sights, sounds, of that old north shore farm that came back like the faint appealing voices of ghosts heard long ago many shadowy years agone.

The soothing nostalgia of copying the old journal seems to have been at least in part therapeutic, given Montgomery's anxiety at the time over her husband. But this diary and the long commentary that follows it are also a way of talking about her own artistic identity: her vivid imagination, the power of memory and recollection, her love of beauty, her fascination with storytelling, and her appreciation of Macneill's authentic, "artless" narrative.

Charles Macneill's diary is of the same rural island history that Montgomery knew, and which she depicts in her novels. Her transcription of this diary, followed by her extended composition on the memories it evokes, can be read as an exploration of her own unique "mind's eye" and her ability to reconstruct atmospheric scenes and settings in her imagination. This volume will provide new insight into Montgomery's evaluation of her own creative process and artistic lineage, at a time when her domestic life was very troubled.

Copy of Diary Kept by Charles Macneill, farmer, of Cavendish, P.E. Island in the years 1892–[1898][1]

"Sunday, Aug. 7, 1892

Came to Charlottetown. Went to Zion Church. Heard Mr. Brewster, Methodist minister, preach a sermon on The Great King, the Lord Jesus."

"Monday, Aug. 8

Went to see Dr. Taylor about my eye. He said he thought it a —[2] and did not operate on it but told me to come back whenever I felt it sore. It does not feel well to-day."

"Monday, Aug. 8

Took the cars at Charlottetown for Hunter River at 3 o'clock Standard Time. Had a nice drive on the cars. Met a Mr. Alex Bernard of Richibucto in town. Came out on the train with him. He left his vessel and went home by steamer. I walked home from Hunter River. Got home about 10 o'clock."

"Tuesday, Aug. 9, 1892

At home to-day. Poor weather for hay-making. Raining hard this afternoon."

"Wednesday, Aug. 10

Fine day. Cut the hay seed in the forenoon. Put hay in in the afternoon. Put up a stack. Did not finish it."

---

1   Charles Macneill (1831–1908) was the father of L.M. Montgomery's friend and cousin Alec Macneill. In her journal of 1925, L.M. Montgomery copies by hand his entire journal, with a few notes of her own.

2   Here LMM inserts a dash, perhaps to indicate she could not read the diagnosis.

"Thursday

Rain to-day. Sent and got 3 deal to fix the horse-stable floor. Paid 63 cts. for them. Got 2 bundles of shingles for Albert. Paid $1 per 100."

"Friday, Aug. 12

Poor weather for haying. Trying to stump. Beginning of storm. George Mackay's schooner is ashore at Rustico."

"Saturday, Aug. 13

Storm not over. Going to try the stumping."

"Sunday, Aug. 14

Preaching at Rustico to-day. Commenced to rain at 12 o'clock to-day with thunder. The people got caught in the rain coming home from church. My eye does not feel well to-day. Is very sore by times. Louisa Donald and her boy were here to-day. They were great strangers. Donald Smith of Clinton and his wife were here to-day."

"August 15

Raining hard to-day. Very poor weather for wheat and hay. My eye is very sore."

"Monday, August 16

Rain all day."

"Tuesday, August 17

Stumping."

"Wednesday, August 18

Cut hay down on road. Put up a stack of hay in Montana for Alexander."

"Thursday, Aug. 19

Commenced harvest. Cut 2 ¼ acres of mixed feed."

"Friday

Albert went to Kensington after Binder Twine. Got 50 lb. at 13 cts. per lb. $6.50."

"Saturday, Aug. 20th.

Very dull weather. Stumping in forenoon. Cutting round field of oats in afternoon.

"*Sunday, Aug. 21*

Went to hear Mr. Allan Simpson preach on behalf of Halifax College. He says we ought to help. Expects this congregation to give twenty dollars. My eyes are very sore to-day. Alexander and Pensie and Maud[3] went to the English church to-day. Mrs. James Craswell and Mary Ellen Mutch was here to-day. Wind north east. Prospect of storm. A lot of grain ripe both oats and wheat. Minnie and Lorenzo was here to-day."

"*Monday, August 22*

Fine clear day for harvest cutting. Wheat up at the back field pretty fair crop. Machine doing fairly well. Eye very sore."

"*Tuesday, Aug. 23*

Cutting oats. Doing well so far."

"*August 23, 1892*

Fine bright day. Going to try and finish cutting oats."

"*Wednesday, Aug. 24*

Finished cutting the field of oats. Moved the binder over to Albert's. Cut his field of oats."

"*Thursday, Aug. 25*

Finished cutting Albert's oats. Taking in the mixed feed."

"*Friday, Aug. 26*

Alexander went to Kensington for deck springs. Did not get them. Got 2 balls of twine. I cut around the field on the road. Very cold."

"*Saturday, Aug. 27*

Cut Albert's wheat. Put in oats. Not very dry."

"*Sunday, Aug. 28*

Rain to-day at preaching. Albert and Alexander heard Mr. Spurr preach."

"*Monday, Aug. 29, 1892*

Cleared up fine. Going to cut the field of oats on the road farm. Don't expect to have a good time at it."

"*Tuesday, Aug. 30*

Fine day. Finished cutting the field on the road at noon. Came home and mowed around the wheat field and started the binder."

---

3   Pensie and Alec Macneill, Charles Macneill's daughter and son. The "Maud" here is LMM.

"Wednesday, Aug. 31

Finished cutting the wheat and stooked it up complete and mowed ½ acre of new land. Took in three loads of oats. Not too dry."

"Sept. 1

Rain this forenoon. Wet the grain pretty bad. Cleared up this afternoon. Fine. Blowing hard from westward. Expect to cut some oats this evening if all goes well."

"Sept. 2

Blowing hard from north-west. Finished cutting the Norway Oats. Taking in grain from Albert's this afternoon. My eye is very sore by times."

"Sept. 3

Fine day for the grain. Blowing hard from the South-west. Taking in oats from the road farm. Afternoon taking in wheat from the old place. Left a lot out. Not quite dry."

"Sept. 4

Beautiful day. Preaching in Cavendish to-day. Mr. Archibald preached from Deuteronomy, 32 chapter + 11th verse. As an eagle stirreth up her nest, fluttereth over her young, spreadeth abroad her wings, taketh them, beareth them on her wings. Oliver Bernard and Lily and Laura was here to-day. Lorenzo Toombs and Minnie and baby was here to-day also."

"Monday, Sept. 5, 1892

Got up at 2 o'clock A.M. Looks very like rain. Commenced to take in wheat. Got finished taking in wheat at four o'clock P.M. Commenced to rain, then cleared up again."

"Tuesday, Sept. 6

Went up to Stanley to the tailor's. Left my suit at Nicholson's to get made. Price to be 6 dollars. Murray Robertson was around to see what could be raised for Mr. Archibald's salary."

"Wednesday, Sept. 7

Cutting oats for Albert with the Binder. Fine day. A fine crop. Russell raked the wheat land and took in the rakings.

"Thurs. Sept. 8

Fine day. Cut the barley by the old house. Mowed the marsh. Pretty good crop.

James Simpson and Robert Brown was here trying to work up more salary for Mr. Archibald. Can't do it at present."

"Friday, Sept. 9.

Topt a hay stack for Albert. Set the mill for to thrash. Going to take in hay. Eye very sore to-day."

"Saturday, Sept. 10

Fine day. Threshed 8 bushels of barley. It grew by the old house. Also threshed 30 bushels of Norway oats from 20 stooks and some rakings. Very good indeed. Better than I expected this year."

"Sunday, Sept. 11

Very fine day. Sacrament of the Lord's Supper at New Glasgow. Albert and Ma was over, also Minnie and Lorenzo Toombs was there. Preaching at N. Rustico in the evening. My eye is very sore to-day. So bad that I can hardly stand the pain. Seems hard to be afflicted thus."

"Monday, Sept. 12

Fine day. Took in the last of Albert's oats. Going to thrash after supper. George Macneill was over after the champion machine to mow his oats. Got it started."

"Tuesday, Sept. 13, 1892

Fine day. Do not feel well to-day. Eye very sore. Hauling old longers for firewood. The rest of the crowd threshing oats at Albert's. Flies very cross. Horses hard to work with. Went down to Rustico this evening to try and collect some bills. Had poor success. The fishermen won't or can't pay. No use to credit them anyhow."

"Wednesday, Sept. 14

Fine day. Putting out manure. Horses hard to work. Flies very cross. Manure not much."

"Thursday, Sept. 15

Fine day. Finished putting out manure. Going to start the plough. Was down at the shore this morning. Bought 3 mackerel from I. Peters. Paid 8 cts. for the 3. He only caught eleven in the boat."

"Friday, Sept. 16, 1892

Very fine day. I am spreading manure to-day. Ma has gone on a cruise to South Rustico. The boys are ploughing down the manure. My eyes are very sore to-day. Getting worse."

"Saturday, Sept. 17, 1892

Fine bright day. Boys ploughing. I am not able to work. My eye is very sore last night and to-day. Wish Dr. Honeywell was home. Lorenzo Toombs was here to-day. He brought a piece of beef. He is very kind. Albert was down at the shore. He bought 3 mackerel. Paid 9 cts. for them. James MacKinstry here this evening. Looking after his cattle that got out of his pasture. The old man is passing away to the land of the leal. Boat sunk at Rustico. One man lost."

"Sunday, Sept. 18

Very fine day. Preaching in Cavendish to-day. My eye is very sore to-day but not so bad as yesterday. Minnie was here to-day. She fetched me a pear. She is very kind to me. Great gale of wind from the west. Everything very dry. Mr. James of Charlottetown is to preach in Rustico, New Glasgow and Hunter River next Sabbath and Mr. MacLeod the Sabbath after in Cavendish at 7 P.M."

"Monday, Sept. 19

Fine day. The boys are ploughing on the old place. Ground very dry and hard. My eye is very sore to-day. I wish Dr. Honeywell would come home. Raining this evening. Wind blowing hard from the north."

"Tuesday, Sept. 20, 1892

Fine day. Cleared up fine after the rain. My eye is very sore. Getting worse all the time. God grant me patience to bear the pain of it. Silvang Peters the peddler was here to-day and two Italians, peddlers selling jewelry. Did not buy any. Abraham Peters was here to-day. The country is full of peddlers. They are a fraud."

"Wednesday, Sept. 21

Find day. Digging potatoes. Started the boiler and parted the sheep and lambs. Poor lambs. Not big. My eye not so sore to-day. Thank God for the respite from pain. Went down to Rustico this evening. Got some fish from Andrew Goatoue. Louis Pinneau and Mosey Peters and Vic Gallant are going on an oyster voyage."

"Thursday, Sept. 22, 1892

Very fine day. Eye not quite so sore today. Made a flake to dry some codfish. Boys ploughing in the old place. I am stumping today. Very hard place. Burning piles tonight. Albert went up to J. Clark's after some money that he owes me. Did not get it. Eye very sore tonight."

"Friday, Sept. 23

Fine day. Boys ploughing in the big field. I am going to stump. Eye sore yet. Stumps very hard to take out. Piles burn finely. Hope to stump more this fall."

"Saturday, Sept. 24

Fine day. Eye sore. Took out big stump in sod field. Went out fishing this afternoon. Had a nice sail but did not get any fish. Sarah sent me a large batch of newspapers. Many thanks for her kindness."

"Sunday, Sept. 25, 1892

A very fine day. Very calm with appearance of rain. Preaching in Rustico this evening. Mr. James is to officiate. Pensie is down at Minnies. My eye is very sore. My sight seems to be getting worse."

"Monday, Sept. 26

Fine day. Hauling wood for boiler. Digging potatoes this afternoon. Good crop. Wallace MacLeod was here looking after Early Potatoes and oats. Eye very sore. Seems to be getting worse."

"Tuesday, Sept. 27, 1892

Fine day. Clearing out the greenhouse. Sent 351 mackerel to the harbor to sell. Alexander goes supercargo. Robert MacKenzie got 3 bushels oats. Sent received from mackerel. Sold to Tenis Buote. $10.87 cts cash."

"Wednesday, Sept. 28

Fine day. Working at the greenhouse. My eye very sore. Can hardly stand the pain of it. Alexander is ploughing sod land along the road."

"Thursday, Sept. 29, 1892

Stumping. It is very hard work. Boys away to the exhibition. Squalls of hail and rain. Turned very cold. Went down to Rustico after potato pickers. Got the promise of three. Bought two potato baskets and one gallon of kerosene oil. Paid 52 cts. for them. My eye is very sore. Losing all hope of it even being better."

"Friday, Sept. 30

Fine day but very windy. Stumping in the forenoon. Digging potatoes in the afternoon. Great crop of Dakota Reds. Going to try and finish them tomorrow. My eye not so sore to-day."

"Saturday, Oct. 1

Fine day but very windy, blowing hard from the northwest and cold. Digging potatoes. Finished the early ones. David Pinneau was here after wood to build a stumping machine. He had some codfish for sale. Gave him flour for them. My eye not quite so sore to-day."

"Sunday, Oct. 2

Fine day with very windy and cold prospects of early fall. 7 o'clock P.M. All the folks off to preaching. May it do them much good for they need to be renewed in the spirit of their minds for they go about to hear or see something new which is soon forgot."

"Monday, Oct. 3

Fine day. Commenced to dig potatoes. Dug 16 loads. Potatoes large but not very plenty. James MacLeod was buried to-day. The admonition is be ye also ready for in such an hour as ye think not the Son of Man cometh."

"Tuesday, Oct. 4

Cloudy with appearance of rain. Dug 19 loads of potatoes. Had to quit early on account of rain. W.T. Sobey of Searletown was here after price of plough. My eye is very sore to-day."

"Wednesday, Oct. 5, 1892

Dull day with showers now and then. Killed a lamb. Put up a fence to keep the horses from eating up the turnips. Dug 1 cartload of potatoes. It has settled down for rain in earnest. Albert was at Laird's mills and fetched home the mixing. Louis Peters got the waggon to go to the harbor with fish. Price to be 15 cts."

"Thursday, Oct. 6, 1892

Find day for digging potatoes. Dug 21 cartloads to-day. Potatoes very large. MacEwen of Stanley was down to-day and bought five old sheep at two dollars each $10. Raining hard tonight. My eye sore."

"Friday, Oct 7, 1892

Fine day. Albert has gone to Stanley with the old sheep. Finished digging potatoes to-day. Had 72 cartloads. Paid Mrs. D. Pinneau for four days work at 45 cts. per day. Amt. $1.80."

"Saturday, Oct. 8.92
Fine day. Digging Albert's potatoes. Dug 28 loads to-day. Paid the French girls off for picking potatoes. Paid $8 for picking potatoes."

"Sunday, Oct. 9, 92
Rainy day. No preaching here to-day. My eye is very sore to-day. Do not appear to get any better."

"Monday, Oct. 10
Cold, windy day. Picking potatoes at Albert's. Finished digging after dinner. Commenced to rake the potato tops this afternoon. Oliver Bernard went to the forge. He broke his mill. Pretty bad smash."

"Tuesday, Oct. 11
Raking potatoes and picking. Got 1 cartload off the field. Sold 1 pelt to the peddler for 55 cts. cash."

"Wednesday, Oct. 12
Very cold windy day. Boys went to plough on the road farm. I was cutting wood and boiling for the pigs. Fixed the back fence. My eye very sore."

"Thursday, Oct. 13
Fine day. Boys finished ploughing on the road. We commenced to plough the potato land. Laird loading the Eddy with potatoes. Price 20 cts. per bushel. Going to haul tomorrow if all is well. Leila was home here and her two children. They appeared to enjoy themselves finely. Went home tonight apples and all."

"Friday, Oct. 14, 1892
Fine day. Hauling potatoes to the harbor. Took 3 loads. Uncle Alexander was here to-day to borrow the machine belt. He is going to start the new threshing machine. John Wedlock was here after the lambs. Price is very slack."

"Saturday, Oct. 15, 1892
Very fine day. Went up to Stanley to-day. John Clark is busy tearing the Brown house to pieces getting it to move. He paid me the bill on the oats. MacLure did not pay me neither did John Sutherland nor Pat MacEwen. Potatoes fetch 23 cts. at Stanely. Got my suit of clothes and a pair of boots for Russell."

"Sunday, Oct. 16, 1892

Fine day. Preaching in Cavendish to-day. Minnie and Ren was here to-day. Ma went down to keep house while Minne went to town. My eye is very sore to-day. Must go and see the doctor as soon as I can."

"Monday, Oct. 17, 1892

Cold day. Wind north. Laird's vessel came into Rustico to-day with coal. Mr. Churchill died last night. Joseph Rogers came after his colt to-day. Pastured it four months. Price $6. David Pinneau was after his plough. Gave him wood for the lend of it. Ren Toombs fetched the clock out of town. Price $1.25. Got a sheare for plough from Joe Robertson. Price 40 cts."

"Tuesday, Oct. 18, 1892

Cold windy day. Picking potatoes after the plough. Albert went to the harbor after coal."

"Wednesday, 19th, 1892

Fine day. Went to New Glasgow. Got the mare shod. Went on to see the doctor. He is going to operate on it. Don't know if he will do it any good. Went down this evening to James Marks looking after some money that he owed me for two years. Did not get it."

"Oct. 20, 1892

Cold windy day with rain. Did not do much to-day. Threshed down at Alberts and moved the mill. No meeting in the church tonight."

"Friday, Oct. 21, 92

Dull day with rain. Threshing wheat. Turned out well. Cleaned 22 bushels. Sent 11 bushels to mill. Paid Albert 11 bushels."

"Saturday, Oct 22, 1892

Dull day. Wind north. Ground very sloppy. Russell has gone to the mill and he is going to get the mare shod. My eye is sore to-day. Cleaned up 21 bushels of mixed feed from 20 stooks of grain. Dan Wedlock was here selling beef. Bought 8 lbs. at 5 cts. per lb."

"Sunday, Oct. 23, 1892

Fine day. Nice and mild. Preaching in Rustico this morning, in Cavendish this evening at 3 o'clock P.M. Minnie and Lorenzo was up to-day. Mr. Archibald preached a missionary sermon. He takes the plea give more."

"*Monday, Oct. 24, 1892*
A dull day with showers. Very rough at night. My eye is very sore. I can get no peace with it."

"*Tuesday, Oct. 25, 1892*
Mild day with showers of rain. Russell went down to Rusticoville with a load of potatoes. Had 18 bushels. Hard road to haul. Joe Gallant is a land shark too greedy to sell anything to."

"*Wednesday, Oct. 26, 1892*
Dull day with appearance of rain. Russell was down to Rustico with a load of potatoes to Tennis Buote. Price is only 20 cts. per bushel. Albert went to Laird's after the grist but did not get it. Was working at the greenhouse to-day. Eye sore yet."

"*Thursday, Oct. 27*
A fine bright day. My eye very sore."

"*Friday, Oct. 28*
A fine day. Ploughing to-day. MacEwen was here to-day after the lambs. Russell was up at Uncle Alexander's picking apples. Got 4 bags full. They are too kind to him."

"*Saturday, Oct. 29*
Very dull day. Working at greenhouse. Dr. Honeywell and Douglas was here to-day. They performed an operation on my eye. Not very sore but do not think they done me any good."

"*Sunday, Oct. 30, 1892*
Very rainy day. Continuous rainpour all day. Wind north east."

"*Monday, Oct. 31*
Fine day. In the house all day. My eye is not very sore to-day. Boys fixing the greenhouse. Getting ready to take up the turnips."

"*Tuesday, Nov. 1, 1892*
Fine day. Boys hauling potatoes to Bayview. Price only 18 cts. Taking up turnips in the afternoon. Great squall of hail tonight."

"*Wednesday, November 2, 1892*
Fine day. Hauled two loads of potatoes to Bayview. Hauled in all 85 bushels.

Taking up turnips."

"Thursday, November 3, 1892
Very sloppy day. Snowed through the night. Raining this morning. Turnips not half out. My eye is very sore to-day. Wrote a letter to Sarah. Going to post it to-day. Nobody travelling. Times very dull."

"Friday, Nov. 4, 1892
Mild day. Taking up the turnips. They are very wet. Not half done. Alexander was up at MacEwen's, Stanley, with ten lambs. The price is to be $1.00 for six, the other four to be $1.17 cts each, in all $14.25. Maxim Peters of South Rustico was here to-day selling beef asking 5 cts. by the quarter."

"Saturday, November 4, 1892
Fine day. Wind north east. Taking up turnips. David Pinneau and Toff Pinneau helping. Eye sore yet."

"Sunday, Nov. 6, 1892
Dull cold day. Wind northeast. Leila and Laura and baby was home to-day. Bell Buntain and Lorne Lepage was here. George Macneill was here last night. My eye not quite so sore to-day."

"Monday, Nov. 7, 1892
Fine day but froze hard last night. Ground did not thaw till noon. Taking up turnips after dinner. Finished at dark. Had 76 loads of turnips. Sent a load to E.C. MacKenzie for good luck. Boys hauled 2 loads of potatoes up to Bayview. Had only 28 bushels out of the 2 loads. Potatoes rotting very fast. Do not expect to have any in the spring. Gave David Pinneau a load for helping with the turnips. Gave Toph Pinneau 1 load of turnips for 1 load of seaweed and 1 day at turnips."

"Tuesday, Nov. 8, 1892
Dull rainy day. Not much doing. Roads very mucky. Expect frost very soon."

"Wednesday, Nov. 9
Fine day. Boys ploughing. I was fixing up for winter. Got the young cattle home. Finished taking up the roots."

"Thursday, Nov. 10, 1892
Fine day. Roads very sloppy. Boys ploughing turnip land."

"Saturday, Nov. 11.

Find day. Froze a little. Albert went to Kensington after brick. Alexander went to Stanley after money. Got some from MacEwen."

"Sunday, Nov. 12
Fine day. Preaching in Cavendish to-day. Ma and Alexander went to William Craswell's funeral but was too late for the burial. Minnie and Ren was here to-day."

"Monday, Nov. 13, 1892
Fine Day. Not doing much. Amelia Buntain was here to-day."

"Tuesday, Nov. 14, 1892
Fine day. I was down at Rustico trying to collect some money but did not succeed. Bought a pair of boots at Tennis Buote's. Paid $1.55. 5 lb. of sugar at 5 1/2 cts., 5 lbs. of sugar at 4 cts."
"Wednesday, Nov. 15
Fine day. Fine weather for time of year. Boys banking house."

"Thursday, Nov. 16, 1892
Fine day. Stumping. Very hard. Do not make much headway."
"Friday, Nov. 17, 1892
Fine day. Alexander and Pensie was in town to-day. Leila was here tonight. Eye sore yet."

"Saturday, Nov. 18, 1892
Fine day. Stumping in forenoon. In afternoon went to Rustico to try and get a man to stump. Got the promise of two Toph Pinneau and Joe Pinneau. Paid Nelson Toombs his bill, $1.14 in full to date."

"Sunday, Nov. 20, 1892
Very rainy day. Nobody went to preaching to-day."

"Monday, Nov. 21
Rainy day. Fixed the bridge this forenoon and killed an ox this afternoon. My eye very sore."

"Sunday, Dec. 4
Preaching in Rustico to-day. Fine day. Sloop went home from Miramichi to-day. The Eddy will likely clear to-day. Wind south west and cloudy. Rain this evening."

"Monday

Fine day with squalls of snow by times. Stumping all day. George R. Macneill was here this evening. Had a pleasant time of it."

"Tuesday, Dec. 6, 1892

Fine day. Ground froze a little. Stumping to-day. Had Sam Pinneau with me in the afternoon. Froze very hard this evening. Ice caught in the bay. Roads very rough now, making very bad travelling indeed. Lent Albert $5. to give Ewen MacEwen in payment of ox."

"Wednesday, Dec. 7, 1892

Dull disagreeable day. Commenced to snow this morning and snowed all day. Hauled the boat home this morning. Sam Pinneau came after Pemac and took him home. Was down at the old barn. Took the sleighs out of stable, box and wood."

"Thursday, Dec. 8, 1892

Fine day. Threshing mixing feed. Pierce Macneill was down after truck waggon to go to town with his pork. Oliver Bernard and Leila was here tonight."

"Friday, Dec. 9, 1892

Rainy day. Cleaning grain to-day. Had 63 bushels from 53 stooks. Pretty good turn out."

"Saturday, Dec. 10, 1892

Fine day for time of year. Busy stumping to-day. Fine time for stumping. Pat MacEwen was down and paid for his hay that he got in 1891."

"Sunday, Dec. 11, 1892

Fine day. Preaching in Cavendish to-day. Was at church to-day with ma and waggon."

"Monday, Dec. 12, 1892

Fine day. Busy stumping."

"Tuesday, Dec. 13, 1892

Fine day. Bushy threshing the oats that grew on the road farm. Finished at eight. Went down to E. MacKenzie's at night. He was in town to-day. He brought home some Jamaica rum. He looks very old."

"Wednesday, Dec. 14

Fine day. Froze a little. Busy stumping all day."

"Thursday, Dec. 15
Fine day. Had Pierce Macneill helping me to kill pigs. Killed four for market."

"Friday, Dec. 16, 1892
Fine day. Albert went to town to-day with the pork. He left at 2 o'clock A.M. Got home at 8 o'clock P.M. Got 6 1/2 cts. per lb. for 1152 lbs."

"December 17, Saturday
Fine day. Doing up the chores and went down to——-with the saws to get sharpened."

"Sunday, Dec. 18
Fine day. Preaching in Rustico. Letty Buntain and Mr. Shaw came here on Saturday night and stayed till after preaching."

"Monday, Dec. 19, 1892
Fine day. Some snow fell last night. Cutting posts and putting them in. Pierce Macneill was down paying for his cask of oil. Kelly was here to-day buying ducks and geese at 6 cents price. He borrowed ten dollars cash to be returned when he comes from town. John Robertson was here with the coal bill. Paid him. Four dollars and 8 cents being the amount of Assess bill."

"Tuesday, Dec. 20, 1892
Fine mild day. Threshing hay-seed this forenoon and cleaning it. Had two and a half bushels. Moved the machine and commenced to thresh wheat. There was two strangers here to-day. They pretended they wanted to trade horses. Doubtful characters."

"Wednesday, Dec. 21, 1892
Cold and blustery. Road not very good for either sleigh or waggon. I threshed and cleaned 20 bus. from 26 stooks. Russell was down at Bernards after stove back. Got a mess of big herring."

"Thursday, Dec. 22nd, 1892
Cold and frosty. Threshing wheat to-day. Roads very bad. Not good for sleigh or waggon."

"Friday, Dec. 23rd
Cold day. Very frosty. Cleaning wheat to-day. Separated 20 bushels of white Fyfe and 2 bushels 2nd class from a bag got in Kensington last spring."

"Saturday, December 24th, 1892

Fine day but very frosty. Roads not very good. Ice caught on the rivers. People crossing Anderson's creek. Alexander was up at Stanley after overshoes for him and Russell. Albert was down at Joe Gallant's with flour. Pensie went down to Minnie's."

"Sunday, Dec. 25th, 1892

Cold frosty day. Preaching in Cavendish to-day. Very few at church. Lorenzo Toombs was here this morning."

"Monday, Dec. 26

Frosty and clear. Roads not good. Threshing wheat to-day. Had Davy Pinneau helping to put away the straw. Gave him a bushel of oats for his pay. Lent Albert 5 dollars to get pine plank at E. Graham's."

"Tuesday, Dec. 27

Fine day but cold. Threshing wheat. I went over to New Glasgow to see Dr. Honeywell. Paid him $7.50 in cash being in full to date."

"Thursday, Dec. 29

Fine day. Putting wheat in granary. Put in 90 bushels of white Fyfe wheat."

"Friday, Dec. 30

Fine day. In town to-day. Bought cloth and shirting for the boys, also saw, axe brace—and—bit. Very bad roads. Came home by the ice. Good roads on the ice."

"Saturday, Dec. 31

Fine day. Busy threshing wheat. Had Sam Pinneau helping me."

"Sunday, Jan. 1, 1893

Very fine day. Preaching in Rustico to-day. Alexander and Pensie was at Rustico. This is my birthday. I am 62 years old to-day. I have been preserved from youth until now. May the Lord guide me by his counsel through this year if I am permitted to see its close. Thou hast been my guide from youth to gray hairs."

"Jan. 2, 1893

Very windy day with heavy rain. Blowing hard from the south east. Cleaned 50 bushels of white Russian wheat. Have the sowing of 6 bushels to thresh yet."

"Tuesday, Jan. 3

Fine day. Threshing wheat. Finished the wheat. Took home Bernard drum and shaker."

"Wednesday, Jan. 4

Cold day. Cleaning the white Russian wheat. Toombs breed. Did not turn out well, only about 6 bushels to one sowed. Not so good as represented."

"Thursday, Jan. 5, 1893

Fine day but cold. Went up to Hillman's forge with thresher. Got two teeth in drum and ballanced. Charged 40 cents. Tillie Macneill was here to-day. Brought a storm."

"Friday, Jan. 6

Blustery day. In woods chopping wood. It is very scattered but we must cut it clean as we go."

"Saturday, Jan. 7

Blustery day. Roads has to be broke. John Laird was round turning the people out. Sawing wood with new saw. Works well."

"Sunday, Jan. 8

Fine day but cold. Preaching in Cavendish to-day. Very few there. Stoves would not burn. Lorenzo Toombs was here to-day. Roads very heavy."

"Monday, Jan. 9

Clear day but frosty. Roads very heavy. Cutting wood in the woods. Poor place. Frank was here to-day after the late Alec Houston's broad-axe."

"Tuesday, Jan. 10

Blustery day. Wind south. It was come to rain yet. Roads very heavy. George and Howard Simpson went up past here at dark on their way out of town."

"Wednesday, Jan. 11, 1893

Fine day. Broke the road opposite this place. Went to the woods after that, cutting firewood and poles. Poor place."

"Thursday, Jan. 12

Fine but very frosty. In woods to-day. Dick Gallant was here to-day after log to make keel for boat 21 ft. long. Paid 80 cts. cash for it."

"Friday, Jan. 13

Fine day but cold. Alexander went down to Joe Gallants. Got a pair of boots.

Cost $4. My money is soon spent. Pensie was down at E.C. MacKenzies getting sewing done on machine. Louis Pinneau got a load of wood."

"Saturday, Jan. 14

Fine day but frosty. Cutting and hauling out wood. Got all the wood but not the poles. Roads very rough."

"Sunday, Jan. 15

Fine day but very chilly. Appears like snow. Preaching in Rustico to-day. Alex and Pensie went down but few went down going to church. Seems to be going out of the fashion."

"Monday, Jan. 16

Fine day but frosty. In woods to-day cutting poles."

"Tuesday, Jan. 17

Fine day but cold. Hauling poles out of woods. Albert up at church cleaning stones. Moved the threshing mill down to Alberts. Sam Pinneau was here after a load of wood."

"Jan. 18

Cold day. Stormy. Boys fixing boiler. Not done much. Time passing away not much done."

"Wednesday, Jan. 18

Fine day but cold. Went to mill with 6 bushels of wheat. Helping to thresh in afternoon."

"Jan. 19

Cold day. Threshing. Mosey Doucette was here selling boots. Albert bought a pair. $3.50. Lent him two dollars cash."

"Jan. 20, 1893

Cleaning wheat to-day for Albert. Went to Rustico in afternoon. Got 2 dollars from Joe Creek. Went on to New Glasgow. Got the harness repaired at French's. Paid one dollar. Leila was here tonight. Went up to hall."

"Saturday, Jan. 21, 1893

Cold blustery day. Ren Toombs was up to-day after ma. Baby very sick."

"Sunday, Jan. 22

Fine day. Preaching in Cavendish to-day. A good many people at church. Albert gone off on a mission I suppose."

"Monday, Jan. 23
Frosty day. In woods cutting firewood. Joe Pinneau was here helping me to-day."

"Tuesday, Jan. 24
Mild day. White frost. In woods to-day cutting wood. Joe Creek and David Pinneau was helping me to-day."

"Wednesday, Jan. 25
Dull day. Heavy white frost to-day. David Pinneau was helping me to-day. Finished cutting the wood. Ren Toombs child died last night."

"Thursday, Jan. 26
Snowing to-day. Heavy fall last night. Ren Toombs child was buried to-day. Roads very heavy. Old Toombs very cranky. Poor man, money is his god."

"Friday, Jan. 27
Cold and blustery day. Roads very heavy. Was down at Ubert Gallant's after a pig. Gave 100 lbs. flour and one dollar cash. Ma not home yet. Nearly as crazy as the Toombs."

"Saturday, Jan. 28
Very frosty day. Roads very heavy. Not much doing. Jack Laird was turning them out to break the roads. Alexander went down to Bernard's to see how the baby is. He came back. Roads very heavy. Baby better. No mail tonight. Russell got 2 gallons of kerosene oil from Pierce. Cost 50 cts."

"Sunday, Jan. 29
Snowing to-day. Roads heavy. Preaching in Rustico to-day. Ma not home yet. She had better stay with the Toombs altogether."
"Monday, Jan. 30
Fine day but cold. Putting out manure. Minnie and Ren Toombs was here to-day. Ma came home."

"Tuesday, Jan. 31
Fine but cold. Threshing at Albert's. Davy and Sam helping."

"Wednesday, Feb. 1, 1893
Cold day. Threshing at Albert's till dinner time. Putting out manure after. Took

a load of wood to E.C. MacKenzie's."

"Thursday, Feb. 2, 1893

Frosty day with high wind. Putting out manure. Albert went to mill in fore-noon. To Joe Gallant's after dinner for laths."

"Friday, Feb. 3

Very frosty day. Not much doing. Cleaning oats for Albert afternoon."

"Saturday, Feb. 4

Cold day with lots of loose snow. Weather looks bad. Boys sawing wood. Going to haul as soon as roads are broke."

"Sunday, Feb. 5

Very cold day. Nobody at church from here. Roads bad."

"Monday, Feb. 6

Fine day but cold. Jack Laird was here warning out to break the roads. Hill very bad. Zebedee Gallant was here looking after flour on credit. Let him have 23 1/2 lbs. Took in a stack of hay from Albert's place."

"Tuesday, Feb. 7

Snowing. Roads heavy. Joe Pinneau after load of straw. Cleaning oats at Albert's. Mrs. Fleming was here to-day. John Fleming gone to hospital."

"Wednesday, Feb. 8

Fine day but cold. Hauling manure. Oliver Bernard was here to-day."

"Thursday, Feb. 9

Fine day. Hauling manure. Pensie gone to E. MacKenzie's to get some sewing done. Got an invitation to A. Rolling's party. Albert hauling laths from Joe Gallants."

"Friday, Feb. 10

Rainy day. Roads bad. Moved up the mill this morning. Nothing doing to-day."

"Saturday, Feb. 11

Fine mild day. Busy threshing norway oats."

"Sunday, Feb. 12

Very fine day. Preaching in Rustico to-day. Alexander and Pensie went there. Russell went to the Baptist."

"Monday, Feb. 13

Fine day. Cleaning oats. D. Pinneau was here and got 2 trees of hardwood at $1.75 cts. Dan Ross and Hen. MacMillan was here with subscription for Church. Gave fifteen dols. Joe Doucette carpenter was here to-day. He fetched a window for granary. Cost eighty cents. Paid him in full."

"Tuesday, Feb. 14

Fine day. Threshing oats. Had Louis Pinneau helping us."

"Wednesday, Feb. 15

Cleaning oats all day. Very mild. Roads very soft. Oliver Bernard was after sleigh to haul mud."

"Thursday, Feb. 16

Colder. Two butchers here from town after fat cattle. J. Clark hauling house. Went through the ice. Went down to Rustico with flour to Doucette and Gallant. Got shoe on mare. Cost 20 cts. Bought a bag of salt, 75 cts, 20 lbs of sugar 90 cts. 2 lbs. of tea 50 cts., Broom 25 cts. in all $2.40."

"Friday, Feb. 17, 1893

Very cold day. Not much doing. Louis Pinneau was up to-day with sleigh of Albert's."

"Saturday, Feb. 18

Fine day but cold. Busy threshing. Finished to-day. David Pinneau was here to-day. Oliver Bernard was here. Alexander has gone to Cavendish Road to get muzzle for horse. Albert has gone on a mission to the Scotch. Russell has been driving Clara about the roads tonight."

"Sunday, Feb. 19

Fine day. Preaching in Cavendish to-day. Minnie was home to-day. Robert Buntain and Oliver Lepage was here to-day. Tillie Clark in church to-day. Not so bad hurt as reported."

"Monday, Feb. 20

Snow to-day. Killed an ox to-day. Cleaned oats after that. Ma went to Davy Jack after a girl for Minnie. Albert was at the forge to-day. Albert was mad because they went by the Cavendish road. It spoiled his trip to John Moffat's."

"Tuesday, Feb. 21st

Stormy this forenoon. Cleaned oats to-day. Had paper from Robby to-day. He says they have 2 ft. down."

"Wednesday, Feb. 22
Fine day. Hauling wood. Took a load of wood to Alexander M. Macneill's. Got a basket of apples. Kind. Alexander gone to mill with Barrister."

"Thursday, Feb. 23
Stormy day. High wind. Nothing doing. Roads heavy."

"Friday, Feb. 24
Cold day. Roads heavy. Hauling manure to Gartmore Farm."

"Saturday, Feb. 25
Fine day but cold. Alexander and Russell went over to the doctor about his hair. Gave him some salve. I went down to Bernard's this afternoon. Took 2 bushels of wheat and a chunk of beef. Oliver is hauling mud. Expects to be rich soon."

"Sunday, Feb. 26
Fine day. Preaching in Rustico this morning. Alexander and Pensie went to the Baptist church this forenoon. The rest went to Cavendish church tonight. Very fine."

Feb. 27. Monday. 1893
Cold and blustery. Boys hauling ice. Had Macaulay helping. Hauled 11 loads to-day."

"Tuesday, Feb. 28
Fine day. Hauled 8 loads to-day. Finished this evening. Paid Macaulay one dollar and 40 cts."

"March 1
Mild day. Hauling poles till noon. Put Maria in sleigh tonight."

"Thursday
Cold and drifty. Hauling manure."

"Friday, Mar. 3
Cold day. Roads heavy. Alec and Pensie took Selena Robinson down to Rustico."

"Saturday, Mar. 4

Fine day. Cutting poles. Pierce and John Fraser was here to-day. Bought 6 bushels of wheat at 80 cts. per bushel. James Mackay was here to-day. Looks well."

"Sunday, Mar. 5
Fine day. Preaching in Cavendish."

"Monday, March 6
Fine day. Hauling manure."

"Tuesday, March 7
Cold with high wind. Cutting poles."

"Wednesday, Mar. 8
Mild day. Cutting poles. David Pinneau was here to-day with 3 fishing checks $10. Sarah Jack was here to-day."

"Thursday, March 9
Fine day. Cutting poles and hauling. Alex. Miller of Rustico was here to-day. He bought 6 bushels of wheat at 80 cts. per bushel. Very low for wheat."

"Friday, March 10
Fine day. Lilla and children were home to-day. Ben Buntain was here tonight."

"Saturday, Mar. 11
Fine day. Boys hauled 4 loads of mud from Island. Albert was up at Kensington after brick and lime."

"Sunday March 12
Fine day. Preaching at Baptist church to-day. Looks like a thaw."

"Monday, March 13
Soft day. Roads very soft. George Gallant of South Rustico was here to-day. Bought ten bushels of wheat. He paid 80 cts. per bushel."

"Tuesday, March 14
Mild day. Roads bad. Cutting poles in woods to-day."

"Wednesday, March 15
Fine day. Boys hauling mud. Ma went down to Ren Toombs to-day. I am very tired. Too much to do."

(Here there is a gap. Either Charles Macneill kept no diary until 1896 or, as is more likely, the notebook was lost or destroyed.)

"January 14, 1896
In Charlottetown on the Grand Jury. There is 12 criminal cases on the docket. Some of them very hard ones."

"Jan. 29
Cleaned 50 bushels of Norway oats and sixteen tailings. Pierce Macneill and wife was here tonight. 12 o'clock. Very fine."

"Jan. 30
Hauled oats from the old barn and threshed them."

"Jan. 31
Cleaned 70 bushels and put them in shop. Alexander off to basket social at New Glasgow Hall."

"Feb. 1, 1896
Helped Albert clean his wheat. Had about sixty bushels from 4 sowed of white chaff. Afternoon sawed wood and threshed 2 rallys of oats. Went down to E.C. MacKenzie's in the evening. Had a pleasant time."

"Sunday Feb. 2
Stormy day. Nobody went to church to-day. Snowing very thick. Roads very heavy."

"Feb. 3
Killing pigs to go to town. Lorenzo Toombs and Mr. George was here to-day. He talked politics most of the time he was here. Did not say anything about religion or the one thing needful. Lelia and her three children came up this evening."

"Feb. 4
Boys in Charlottetown to-day. Had 827 lbs. of pork. Got 5 cts. per lb. and 50 cts. over. Forty-one dollars and eighty-five cents. Had two cow-hides that weighed 96 lbs. at 4 1/2 cts. per lb. Came to four dollars and thirty 2 cts."

"Feb. 5
Went down to Rustico to-day to get barrel hooped at Mathew's but he had no hoops to fix it with. Went on to Rollings. Quill was in town. Old John Rollings was keeping house. Bought a new barrel and left the old one to be repaired. The boys are off to Ren Toombs. Minnie has a quilting party to-day. Tom Pin-

neau was around to-day begging for Henry Mac————. His wife is very sick and takes fits."

"Friday, Feb. 6

Threshing oats. Very fine day. Aquila Rollings was here with a barrel that he hooped. Also a new one. Gave him one dollar for them."

"Feb. 7

Cleaning oats all day. Had 100 bushels and 20 bushels second class. Alex Stewart was after his pig. Alfred Macneill was here with a sow of George Macneill's. Silver thaw last night. Soft to-day."

"Feb. 8, 1896

Stormy in forenoon. Busy threshing in afternoon. Chesley Clark and Gertie Macneill came here at 9 o'clock."

"Sunday, Feb. 9

Fine day. The crowd went down to Rustico church in morning up to Cavendish church in evening. Lorenzo Toombs and Walter Buntain and Bessie was here tonight, also Long Five Axe Handles."

"Feb. 10

Stormy day. Not doing much. Expect to thresh tomorrow if all is well and finish the oats."

"Feb. 11

Fine day. Finished threshing oats. Cleaned it in afternoon and put in granary. Had sixty-five bushels and lots of tailings."

"Feb. 12

Threshing wheat to-day. George and Ronald Matheson was here to-day trying to buy wheat. Offering 75 cts. per bushel. Expect to go at the wood tomorrow. Russell after Paul Gallant."

"Feb. 13

Fine day. Cutting wood. Had Paul Gallant with me."

"Feb. 14

Stormy day. Duncan Ferguson storm—stayed here till Monday."

"Feb. 15

Cold day. Cleaning wheat. Had 60 bushels. Put 44 bushels in granary and 12 bushels in barn and 4 in shop. Jack Laird was here to-day turning them out to break the roads. Crazy as a foole."

"Feb. 16 Sunday

Stormy. Went to church. Heard Mr. George preach. His text was Whatsoever thy hand findeth to do do it with thy might. Went down to Albert's this afternoon. Mr. Ferguson and I had our teas there."

"Monday, Feb. 17

Cold day. Working about the barn. Ferguson went home after dinner."

"Tuesday, 18th

Cold day. Threshing wheat all day. L—Lepage and Ida and Maria Buntain came here tonight. Went up to Pierce Macneills but did not find them home. Went down to Ren Toombs to help Minnie hook."

"Wednesday, 19th

Fine day. Went after coal. Got 320 lbs. of coal, 60 cts., 1/2 gallon Linseed oil 37 cts."

"Feb. 20

Stormy day. Cleaning wheat all day in the barn. Did not carry it up in granary to-day. Alexander went down to Toombs after the girls. Roads very bad. Russell went up to Hillman's to prayer meeting tonight. Collecting for Foreign Missions. Gave 2 dollars and 30 cts. Stan Wedlock was here tonight."

"Feb. 21st

Carrying wheat to granary. Alexander went to mill. Took a grist and fetched one home. Russell took the girls up to Robertson's this afternoon after that went to Pierce Macneill's."

"Feb. 22

Threshing White Chaff wheat. Finished the threshing. Mice very bad. Paul Gallant was here to-day. He got 102 lbs. of flour at 2 1/2 cts. per lb. David Pinneau was here. He got 200 lbs. of hay at 2 25 cts. per lb."

"Feb. 23

Very fine day. Our folk went to the Baptist church in morning to Stanley in afternoon. I went down to Ren Toombs in the evening. W. Houston was there and Oliver Bernard and family. Roads very heavy."

"Feb. 24

Fine day. Threshing clover seed. Poor turnout, almost a failure. David Pinneau fetched up his calf. James Elliott was here after wheat. Jim Bulman and Nelson Orr trying to get up a Pie social at New Glasgow. Alexander has got the yellow mare. He pretends that he is going to Ren Toomb's but it is very likely he has gone on a mission to the Scotch."

"*Feb. 25*

Cold and blowy. Alexander gone to town with Ren Toombs. Pork. Got 5 cts. per lb. and one dollar over. Came to $77.15. Cleaning wheat in barn all day."

"*Feb. 26, 1896*

Cold day. Went to woods to-day. Cutting wood. Broke the road to woods and hauled some."

"*Feb. 27th*

In woods cutting wood. Hard work keeping sleighs going."

"*Feb. 28*

Cutting wood all day. Had Mosey with me all day and Paul half day. Very fine. Alex not very smart. Too much pie social at New Glasgow last night. Too much bushel for a small canoe."

"*Feb. 29*

Soft day. Finished taking out the wood. Russell gone to Rustico with the girls. Rather big for his pants. Duncan Ferguson was here to-day with his grinding machine. It is very likely that it is a patent swindle."

"*March 1*

Fine day. Our folk gone to church. Sarah Jack came here last night looking after stray. Ren and Minnie and children here to-day. Too late to go to church. Minnie seems cross about it."

"*Mar. 2*

Soft day. Putting out manure. Commenced to rain in evening."

"*Mar. 3*

Soft day with thick fog. Roads bad. Busy separating wheat. Russell was down at Albert's. He is sick. No mail tonight. Crewe is a slow coach."

"*Mar. 4*

Cold and blustery. Wind north."

"Mar. 5

Cold and windy. Hauling out manure to back field."

"Mar. 6

Cold and blustery. Nothing doing."

"Mar. 7

Fine day. Hauling out manure. Walter Buntain was here to-day. He bought 10 bus. of white Fyfe wheat. Albert and Bessy was here tonight. Bob and Milton MacKenzie was here to-night."

"Mar. 8

Fine day. Alexander and Pensie gone to Rustico church. Albert and Bessy gone to New Glasgow to see Dick."

"Mar. 9

Helped Albert to kill his pigs. They weighed 270 lbs. 268 and 234. Jonas Doucet of Winslow road was here to-day. He bought Ten bushels of White Chaff wheat at $1 per bushel."

Mar. 10

Albert went to town to-day with his pork. Got 5 cts. per lb. and 35 cts. over. We were hauling dulse to-day from the old place."

"Mar. 11

Fine day. We were hauling dulse in the forenoon. Turnips in afternoon from pit. Kept well. Albert was here tonight. He got an offer for his cattle. 80 dollars. Did not think it enough. Could not get any more."

"March 12

Stormy day. Clearing up at noon. Russell not very sound. Been out very late last night, poor boy. Alex. fixing his harness. Going on a mission. 2 Italian peddlers here to-day. Bought 2 pair of pants for 3 dollars . . ."

"March 13

Cold day. High wind. Boys hauling poles from old place. I was down at E.C. MacKenzie's. He is as proud as Lucifer. Lecture at the hall tonight. Poor trade."

"March 14

Fine day. Hauling in hay. Hugh Cousins was here and fixed the pump. He charged one dollar and thirty cents. Gave him one dollar and ten cents and oats for rest."

"*Sunday 15, March*

Fine day. Mr. Sutherland of Charlottetown preached to-day. Text John 17th and 9 verse. Minnie was up to-day. She drove herself up with Tom. Found a whip. Very nervous."

"*March 20*

Rainy with high wind and roads very bad. Not very good prospects for the big Tea Squall in the manse. Poor Lucy will burst herself. Was down at old barn. Put in the boards. Fixed up the barn floor ready to sell hay. George Macneill was down at E.C. MacKenzie's Friday evening. Roads very bad. Not many at tea. They realized 18 dollars. Expect to make more on Monday evening. It is doubtful."

"*March 21st*

Froze hard last night. Busy separating White Fyfe wheat. Cleaned 10 bushels. Put in shop. Bessy was up. Mrs. E.C. MacKenzie was up this afternoon about the farm. Hard night from every point of view. Wants lots of fencing. Can't save crop without fence."

"*March 22*

Fine day. Appearance of soft weather. Was at Baptist church to-day. Heard Mr. Spurr preach a sermon on part of Lord's prayer. Thy kingdom come on earth. Russell gone to drive Mr. George to Stanley. Alex and Pensie went to Rustico church. Gone to dine at Ren Toombs. Mean. Letty Buntain and Eddy Coles came here to-day and stopped here all day. Went up to manse tonight and hall. Was down at E.C. MacKenzie's to-day."

"*March 23*

Bargained for the farm on shares for five years with privilege of buying if sold. Have a lot of poles to cut for the place."

"*March 24*

Cutting poles for home place. Cut 256 Poles. Hard place."

"*March 25*

Cutting poles on MacKenzie place. Hard place to cut. Lots needed. Ed Coles was here to-day to exchange oats. Had 103 lbs. of oats. Mr. Murphy of Mill Vale was here after hay. Got 573 lbs. Gave me 2 dollars. 73 lbs. not paid for. Mrs. Harker and Mrs. Murray was here tonight. Alex went home with them."

"Mar. 26

Cutting poles on MacKenzie place. Davy Pinneau and Louis Pinneau and I working hard. Boys hauling poles. Murphy back after hay. Lew Blacquier got 354 lbs."

"March 27

Soft day. Cutting poles on MacKenzie place. Boys putting out manure. Alex off on a mission tonight."

"March 28

Fine day but cold. Cutting poles on MacKenzie's place. Tillie Clark was here to-day. Smart."

"Mar. 29, Sunday

Fine day. At church. Heard Mr. George preach from lst Peter, 3rd chapter and 15th verse. Sanctify the Lord in your hearts and be ready always to give an answer to every man that asketh of you a reason for the hope that is in you with meekness and fear. Heard that Mr. Archibald has made a demand on the congregation for $157 with 3 dollars int. Poor human nature. Alex and Pensie gone down to Ben's. Ren Toombs here to dinner to-day."

"Mar. 30

Fine day. Cutting poles on MacKenzie place. Most tired of it. Wished I had not anything to do with it. Better to have invested my money somewhere else."

"Mar. 31

Heavy fall of snow. Boys at work at Mack place. Ren Toombs was up with a pig that he bought from Tennis Buote. Price $12.00. Alexander gone with a load of straw to Jacks. Price $1.25."

"April 1

Blustery. Alex and Pensie went to New Glasgow. Pensie got her tooth pulled. Oliver Bernard was here to-day. Hauling hay this afternoon. Louis Pinneau was here. Paid him off."

"April 2, 1896

Was in Charlottetown to-day. Fine roads in morning. Nearly all bare at night. Paid Credit Foncier Society for E.C. MacKenzie 65 dollars and 33 cts. Also bought 50 lbs. clover seed. Cost $16."

"April 3

Stormy day. Not much doing. Going to haul hay as soon as fine."

"April 4

Fine day. Hauling hay to-day. Alexander put Maggie in sleigh. Went well. Jack also went well."

"Easter Sunday, April 4

Fine day. Ma went to Baptist church to-day. Good roads. Ren Toombs was here after Minnie and children. Alex and Pensie going to Rustico church. Russell appears not to know where he is going. Poor fellow."

"April 5

Fine day. Hauling manure to lower field. Good roads. Ma and Bessy preparing to go to Robertson's on a cruise. Joe Pinneau was here to-day pretending to buy wheat. Ren Toombs was here again after his pig. Did not take it home. He bought 12m of shingles at 1.75 per M. Boys off to Rustico to meeting. Come home in good time. That's right."

"April 6

Fine day but cold. Cutting poles on MacKenzie place. Murphy of Mill Vale was here after hay. William MacKay was here. Got 300 lbs. of hay and bag of potatoes. Toph Pinneau was after wood. $1. Dugald Henry was here to-day. Oliver Bernard got a load of straw. Mrs. Flemming was after straw."

"April 7

Cold day. Cutting poles on MacKenzie farm. Russell hauling poles out to field."

"April 8

Fine day. Hauling poles."

"April 9

Fine day. Cutting poles in forenoon down at E.C. MacKenzie's. This afternoon he sined an agreement for his farm for five years on halves."

"April 10

Down on road farm cutting scantling."

"April 11

Fine day. Snow going fast. Boys hauling scantling home. Russell at mill this morning. Fetched home a grist of flour. Alexander gone after Mosey Gallant to hew scantling. No mail tonight."

"April 12, Sunday

Fine day. Our folks gone to prayer meeting. May it do them good. Not many there. Roads passable."

"April 13
Dull day. In woods in forenoon. Hewing scantling at door. Sold 434 lbs. of hay to Mosey Doirong. Dora out on ice after seals."

"April 14
Hewing scantling and fixing roller. Cold Easterly wind."

"April 15
Cutting poles. I don't think we have enough."

"April 16
Fine day. Sawing wood. Sharpening pickets at home and hauling poles at home."

"April 18
Sawing wood and sharpening pickets."

"April 19
Dull day. Ice nearly all gone. Children gone to Baptist church. Mr. Spurr had good text but poor delivery. Can't help that. Russell gone to Darnley Clark's. Poor boy."

"April 20
Fine day. Wind west. Ground drying up fast. Sharpening pickets on MacKenzie place and hauling dulse in afternoon."

"April 20
Fine day. Commenced to fence on MacKenzie place. Frost not all out. Lots of work."

"April 21st
Fine but cold. Fencing on Mack place. Bob Robert bought 3 old sheep. Price 15 dollars."

"April 22
Heavy white frost. Going to fence on Mack place."

"April 23
Hard frost last night. Fencing on Mack place. Can't get along. Too much frost.

Hugh McLure was after wood to make swingle trees."

"April 24

Cold day. Wind north. Ice on shore. Fencing on Mack place back of house."

"April 25

Fine but cold. Wind north. MacKenzie very poorly. We are putting up barbed wire fence for pasture."

"April 26

Fine day. Preaching in Cavendish to-day. Our folk gone to church. May they hear something that will do them good. I am at home alone, cooking."

"April 27

Fine day. Fencing on MacKenzie place. Got 119 lbs. of barbed wire and 7 lbs. of staples from George Macneill. Put it up. Did not have enough to be returned."

"April 28

Fine day. Fencing on line shore. Made a good job."

"April 29

Cold. Wind north. Blowing hard. Very high sea. Was down at Ewan MacKenzie's. He is very sick. Don't think that he will live long, poor man. Alexander took down a load of wood and stayed till 12 o'clock."

"April 30

Very cold day for time of year. Wind northeast and froze. High tides. Fishermen expect to lose their nets."

"May 1

Cold day. High wind. Ground hard froze. Alexander making brooms. Russell gone down to MacKenzie's."

"May 2

Cold day. High wind. Not much doing. MacKenzie very low. Louis Blacquiere after hay. Got 365 lbs., gave cash 45 cts."

"May 2

Fine day. Fixed the dulse road. Sold 2 loads of hay at 50 cts. per 100 to L. Fraser and Sam Woolner. E.C. MacKenzie died to-day at eleven o'clock. Took down a load of wood to them this evening."

"May 3

Very fine day. Begins to look like spring. Russell and Chesley Clark off to New Glasgow road. Albert and Bessy off to New Glasgow. Preaching in Cavendish tonight."

"May 4

Cold. Northeast wind with rain. E.C. MacKenzie was buried to-day. Large funeral. 45 wagons there. Oliver Bernard and Lelia was up here. Chesley Clark went home. Ma very sick with her stomach."

"May 5

Fine day. Fencing on MacKenzie farm all day. Turned very cold."

"May 6

Hauling dulse this morning."

"May 7

Hauling dulse. Alex off to Roberts with fat sheep. $15.00. Rolling down piece of land on MacKenzie place. All weeds."

"May 8

Putting out manure on lower field."

"May 9

Putting out manure."

"May 10

Preaching in Cavendish to-day. Mr. George gone home on business."

"May 11

Fine day. Ploughing sod land by factory."

"May 12

Ploughed land at factory."

"May 13

Fine but cold. Ploughing."

"May 14

Planted corn and potatoes and sowed mixed grain. Wheatley here looking after fat cattle. Did not sell."

"May 15

Sowed 7 bushels of mixed feed and 4 bushels of wheat on MacKenzie place."

"May 16
Sowed 11 bushels of oats on field by road."

"Sunday, May 17
Fine day but dark. Looks like rain. Uncle James was here to-day."

"June 5
Finished planting potatoes."

"June 6
Fencing on MacKenzie place."

"June 7, Sunday
Fine day but cold."

(Here occurs another gap. The Diary resumes on Saturday, February 6, 1897.)

In Charlottetown to-day. Paid off the loan society for MacKenzie's farm and lifted the mortgage but did not pay for the satisfaction. Papers amount to about $4 in the registry office.

"Sunday, Feb. 7
A fine day. Preaching in Rustico to-day. Pensie gone down this morning. Off to Stanley this afternoon. At Cavendish tonight. Russell in Town yesterday. Off with Chesley Clark last night. Did not show up to-day. Poor fellow. Seems off his base."

"Monday, Feb. 8
Fine day. Soft. Taking in stack of hay. Oliver Bernard and family was up here to-day."

"February 9
Fine day. Social in hall tonight in aid of E.J. MacKenzie. Realized about 40 dollars. Not too bad for him."

"Feb. 9
Cold day. Hauling out manure. Marie Buntain and Ida Lepage went home this morning."

"Feb. 10
Fine but cold. Fixing shed door. Hard day."

"Feb. 11

Cold day. Went to the woods to cut poles. Russell came after me. William MacKay was along after 3 loads of hay. Got 3 good loads. Lecture in hall tonight by Mr. Fullerton. Robert Lamont was there and sung some Scotch songs. The people had a good time."

"Feb. 12

Cold day. Threshing oats to-day and cleaning. Mosey Doucet was here with 3 pairs of boots that he mended. Cost $1.50. Mrs. MacKenzie was here to change money to pay Hillman's bill. She also paid me six dollars and 60 cents that she borrowed from me in Town to pay of the Loan Society. So far so good."

"Saturday, Feb. 13, 1897

Fine day but cold. Louis Pinneau was here after wood. Had one dollar to spare. I cut 20 poles to-day. Russell hauled them out. Pensie and Bessy off to Stanley preaching. Hammond Macneill was here. Alexander off on a mission to Milton. Likely to lose his reckoning."

"Sunday, Feb. 14

Fine day. Fred Clark was here after Russell. Preaching in Cavendish tonight. All gone to meeting. I at home."

"Feb. 15, 1897

Fine day. Busy threshing oats all day. Mrs. Cliff here after straw. Sent her a load. Charged her one dollar. Sam Pinneau was here after wood for 25 cents worth. Howard Simpson was here with a pig for the third time. Pensie off to New Glasgow after a dressmaker. Russell gone too. Alexander off to the Baptist Young People's meeting. Albert and Bessy gone to Jericho."

"Friday, Feb. 19

Fall of snow. We are busy cleaning mixed grain. It was badly cut up by rats. Had about 60 bushels of grain. Our crop is all threshed and cleaned. Had a fair crop all round. We ought to be thankful for all the mercies we receive from the giver of all good. He alone can bless us and make us to prosper."

"Feb. 27

A fine day but cold. Sawing wood at the door. Leon Gautier was here after wood. He had no money and his credit is poor. Sam Pinneau of North Rustico was here to-day. He got 492 lbs. of hay at 40 cts. per 100. Will Bulman was here also. Albert was here to-day. Times are very dull this winter. There is no demand for wheat or flour. If markets do not improve farmers will have hard times to meet their bills."

"Feb. 28

Fine day but cold. Roads heavy. No preaching in Cavendish or Rustico nor Stanley. Mr. Robertson gone to help a brother preacher. Was down to Oliver Bernard's. The road from Mrs. Cliffs to Bernards very bad indeed. The Bernard family all sick with cold. Laura is very sick. Hal is doing the work. Harriet and Nina are home from Charlottetown on a cruise for their health. Mag Laird came there through the snow almost done out but crazy as usual. It is a family failing."

"March 1, 1897

Cold day. Very frosty. Roads very heavy. At home. Not doing much. Expect to take in stack of hay tomorrow."

"Mar. 2

Cold and blustery. Roads very bad. Took down a load of wood to Mrs. MacKenzie. She was just out. Her man Mosey is sick. Not able to work. He has a hard time of it. Bad weather and short of grub."

"March 8

Received a letter from James P. Bowden. M.D. Medical Director of the Medical Reserve fund Association, Broadway, New York, No. 305, 307 and 309, making inquiry concerning Albert E. French. Address Walnut Hill, Deothar Mass."

"March 9

Answered the questions asked by Dr. Bowden regarding Albert French and sent them on by mail to his address."

"March 12

Fine day. Roads very soft. Looks like spring. Tennis Doiron was here and bought ten bushels of white chaff wheat at 80 cts. per bushel. Amount Eight dollars. Paid four dollars. The balance of four dollars still due is to be paid in June 1897."
"March 13

Soft day. Roads very bad. In wood cutting poles to-day. Great spree at John Franklin's last night in aid of the (indecipherable word) Famine Fund."

"Sunday, March 14, 1897

Fine day but cold. Froze hard last night. Ren Toombs was here to dinner to-day. Alex sick. Gone off on a mission to the Scotch. Had a cow calved last night. Russell doing up the chores to be ready to go to the Baptist meeting."

"Monday, March 15

Cold blustery day. Boys went to mill this morning. Took 14 bushels of wheat and 21 bushels of mixed grain to be smashed for the fat cattle. Going to pay for the grinding about 3 cts. per bushel."

"Tuesday, March 10

Cold and blustery. Not much doing. Was down at Albert's this morning. Moved down the mill in the evening."

"Wednesday, March 17

Cold day. Nothing doing. Keeping things straight around the barn."

"Thursday, March 18

Fine mild day. Hauling hay in forenoon. Boys went to mill in afternoon. Fetched home a grist of flour and mixed grain. Herbie charged 50 cts. for smashing."

"March 18

George Cudmore and Son and Mr. Younker was here after wheat. They bought 17 bushels at 80 cts. per bushel. Amount $13.60."

"March 19

Fine mild day. Hauling poles out of the woods after dinner. Went down to Rusticoville. Bought 4 M of shingles at $1.00 per M."

"March 20

Went down to Joe Gallant's. Bought 6m of shingles at $1.00 per m."

"Sunday, March 21

Fine day. Preaching in Rustico to-day. Alexander and Ma went to Ren. Toombs for dinner. Charley MacKenzie was here to tea. Albert and Bessy here from New Glasgow."

"Monday, March 22

Fine day. Boys off to the mud. I done up the work and cut 20 poles."

"March 23rd

Sloppy day. Boys hauling mud. I hauled out the manure. Alexander home tonight. Went to Will Rod's after money."

"March 24

Fine day. Boys hauling mud. I done up the chores and went down to the Ferry after oil, sugar and canvass. Cost one dollar and fifty cents cash. Lewie Durrong was here and bought 3 bushels of wheat at eighty cents per bushel. $2.40."

"April 5, 1897
Went up to Stanley to-day. Had very bad roads. Posted a letter to J.A. Simmons Toronto Can. with post office order for the sum of Twenty Dollars for Clover Seed 110 lbs. Alsyke 35 lbs, 2 bushels wheat and 10 lbs. of turnip seed and the ballance if any in white clover seed."

"April 8
Fine day but cold. Nelson MacCoubrey was here to-day with harness that he repaired. Repairs cost one dollar and five cents. Pair of new traces 2 dollars and 15 cts. Took in a pit of turnips. Kept fairly well. A few froze."

"April 9
Fine day. Threshing oats at Alberts. Very much heated. Enough to sicken anybody. Snowed a lot tonight. Did not do much good. Prospect of spring seems to be remote but it will come."

"April 24
Fine day. Putting girth in barn. Had Demos Gallant helping me. Made a good job of it. Went down to Ben Houston's after four bolts to fasten the girth in place. Cost 50 cts. Also had a card from Dan McKinnon, Station Master, regarding seed that come from Toronto. There is $2.38 freight to pay. Raining this evening."

"Sunday, April 25th
Fine day. Preaching in Cavendish to-day. Ren Toombs called in this morning and took Ma to church. Oliver Bernard and Lelia was here to dinner to-day. Mr. Baker is holding meetings in the Baptist meeting house every night. Boys attend regular."

"Monday, April 26
Fine day. I went to Hunter River after my clover seed and wheat and turnip seed. Got them. They seem to have been knocked about very much. The bags are in an emaciated condition. The freight cost 2.38."

"Tuesday, April 27
Rainy day. Pork killed to go to town. Did not get on account of rain."

"Monday, September 27

Came into Charlottetown tonight. Staying at Mr. Coffin's. Bought 3 lbs. of tea at Mr. Moore's at 78 cts and 10 lbs. of sugar, 1 lb. of cakes 8 cts., 1 pair of gloves 65 cts."

"Tuesday, Sept. 28

Went aboard the Princess at 7 o'clock in the morning. Came across to Pictou. Had a rough passage across. Train did not leave until 2 o'clock. Had dinner at Pictou at the Royal. There was a great many people on the cars in to Halifax. Arrived at 8 o'clock. Got lodgings in a private house kept by a Mr. Dyer at 980 Lockman St."

"Wednesday, Sept. 29th

Fine day. Took the street cars and went down to the Exhibition. There is a great show of cattle and grain and there is great attractions. We were on board the big ship Renown and seen her all through. Went to the Exhibition and seen the Seige of Sebastopol and the great diver that jumped from a pole into the water, the soldiers marching and going through their evolutions and lots of side shows."

"September, 30

Went around the city of Halifax. Went and seen the Provincial Exhibition building. Seen the portraits of all the great people of the past time of Halifax and specimens of all the minerals that are found in Canada. Went out and seen the citadel, the fortification, the big old clock and the forts on St. George's Island and MacNab's Island. Seen them blasting the hard rock."

"October 1, 1897

Left at 7.20 for home by express train for Truro. Changed cars for Pictou. Arrived there at 2:25, being 25 mins. late. Got aboard the Princess bound for Charlottetown. George MacNeill got left at Pictou and lost his passage. Had a very rough passage across the straits. Arrived in Charlottetown at Mr. Coffin's at eight o'clock. Met Russell there. Started for home at 9 o'clock. Had a very cold, windy drive home. Called at Joseph Doucets on the Rustico Road. Got warmed and fed. Came on to the bridge. Very big tide. Lot of water on bridge. Found things had gone on pretty well while I was away."

"Saturday, Oct. 2

Went up to Stanley. Bought 6 potato baskets at 10 cts. each, 60 cts. Pair of shoes at $1.50 and 42 lbs. of beef at 5 1/2 cts. per lb."

"*Sunday, October 3*

Fine day. Froze hard last night. Ma went down to see Ben. Alex likes a drive."

"*Thursday, October 7*

Commenced to dig the potatoes. Had 46 loads off home place and 27 loads on Mrs. MacKenzie's place. Wages for picking potatoes cost me eleven dollars."

"*Thursday, October 14, 1897*

Went over to New Glasgow to Mrs. George Houston's funeral. There was three ministers there. Mr. Robertson, Mr. Crawford and Mr. Pickles. There was about 85 wagons in the procession."

"*Sunday, October 17*

Gale of wind from the west that levelled all the fences. Preaching in Rustico this forenoon. The wind does not seem to moderate any yet. Carried our boat across Albert's field and split her plank badly. It will cost something to repair her. If fishing improves I will fix her if not she stays there."

"*Saturday, Oct. 30, 1897*

Fine day but windy. Had Mosey building furnace for boiler. Got a new boiler. Sheet iron. Cost 2 dollars."

"*Sunday, October 31st*

Fine day. Preaching in Rustico. Pensie and Alexander and Will Bulman gone to church. Ren Toombs was here tonight. Ma gone to preaching. Boys both gone."

"*Monday, November 1*

Fine. Taking up the turnips. Had Lucy Gallant helping me. Took up 57 loads."

"*November 4*

Finished taking up the turnips. Took two loads to Mrs. MacKenzie and put them in the cellar and one load to Mrs. Gallant and one bushel of barley for hens. John Wedlock was here and bought 3 lambs at 2 cts. per lb. They weighed 234 lbs. Came to $4.08. Got paid for 115 1/2 bushels of potatoes at 22 cts. per bushel."

"*Saturday, November 6*

Russell was down at Ben Houston's and got his mare shod. Cost 38 cts. Also got harness repaired at Nelson MacCoubrey's."

"Sunday, November 6, 1897

Blustery day. High wind with flurries of snow. Two schooners went down this morning. Supposed to have got out of New London that Dan Wedlock had loaded."

"Monday, November 7

Rainy day. Blustering. Hauling off potato tops. Alexander and Albert gone up to Stanley to get examined by Dr. Dan to see if they are fit to join the Foresters."

"Tuesday, November 8

Fine day. Ploughing all day. Very tired tonight. Russell had about 5 bushels of potatoes that he picked to-day. Fred and Maggy was down this evening. Commenced to rain very hard about 10 o'clock."

"November 9

Squally with showers of rain and sleet. Ploughing potato land. Ground very wet. Ma was down at MacKenzies. They have got the measles."

"November 18, 1897

Cold and wet. Freezing tonight. Put out a lot of manure and spread it. Got it most all ploughed in. Got up the young cattle home this morning. Albert is going to Summerside tomorrow with cheese. Hard time to get help. Have to do without."

"Saturday, November 20th

Threshing mixed grain. Fields are covered with snow."

"Sunday, November 21st., 1897

Preaching in Cavendish to-day. Rough day. Hard time on the sheep. Blowing hard from the southeast with sleet and snow. Wind chopped round to the northwest and blew a gale. Hard time for vessels."

"Monday, Nov. 22

Cold windy day. Roads very hard. Russell went to the mill with 15 bushels of mixed grain. Had to get the yellow mare shod at Hillman's. Cost 40 cts. I was in the woods to-day cutting wood for Mrs. MacKenzie. Cut 3 loads. Takes a lot of chopping of that small wood to make a load. I charge her 75 cts. for the work done. Alexander and Albert off to join the Foresters. They ought to be satisfied now."

"*November 23, 1897*

Fine day. Got home the sheep this morning. 23 all told. Split up the wood and watered the cattle and cleaned up the stables. Fixed the mill-house door. Boys banking house with clay. Walter Buntain was up with a pig. Did not take her home with him."

"*Wednesday, Nov. 24*

Clear cold day. Fixing up the pig house. It is all to pieces. Ought to build a new one next year if able. Cutting wood and fixing up the chores. Boys in at Albert's. He is sick. Done up his work. Went down tonight to saw wood. Russell at mill. Fetched home the mixing and oatmeal. Wedlock was round letting people know that the coal is in."

"*Friday, Nov. 26*

Fine day. Busy threshing oats all day. Had Gilbert Blacquiere cutting bands. Mill goes well. Mice are bad in the grain this year."

"*Saturday, Nov. 27*

Rainy day. Cleaning oats in barn all day. Alexander was ploughing on MacKenzie place in forenoon. Walter Buntain was up with his sow. He took her home with him and left the other one. Me and Gilbert sawed wood for Sunday. Boys took up 200 lbs. of hay to Mr. Robertson and got the mail. Lots of news but not much that concerns us."

"*Sunday, November 28*

A fine day. Froze last night. Roads very fair. Preaching in Rustico to-day. Not many went down. Alexander and Russell went to church and back to Ren Toombs for dinner. Home for to go to Cavendish tonight. Will Bulman was round tonight again."

"*Monday, Nov. 29*

Fine day. Putting out manure in field by barn. Expect to get it ploughed down but I may not. Frank Murphy was here to dinner. He was after the price of the plough that I bought. I paid him 12 dollars in full. He fetched a wheel and clip. Cost 50 cts. Did not pay him. Moved the mill down to McKenzie's barn. Did not set her. Prescott the tax gatherer was round after the school tax."

"*Tuesday, Nov. 30*

Sloppy day. Snowed a good lot last night. It is all slush this morning. Set the mill and fixed up the barn. Put in a barrel at the brook and banked up the brook. Came home and sawed wood after dinner, me and Gilbert. Alexander gone off to Churchill's sale. Did not buy anything. He is satisfied now. Came home and fed his pigs."

"Wednesday, December 1

Cold frosty day. Busy sawing wood at the door and stowing away the farm implements. Not enough room. Got home the ram and left a ram lamb at Albert's. Did not pay for it. Oliver Bernard was up with his imported sow. Alexander was up at A.J. MacLeod's. He got paid for the potatoes that we put on board the schooner at Bay View. 29 bushels and 15 lbs. $7.36."

"Thursday, Dec. 2

Cold day. Fixing up Mrs. MacKenzie's barn ready for threshing. Albert and Russell gone to get their horses shod. Mrs. MacKenzie gone to Stanley with turkeys. There was a funeral at the churchyard to-day. A Mrs. Parkman daughter of the late John Robertson. Arrived at 3 o'clock P.M. from Charlottetown.

Commenced to thresh wheat after dinner. Threshed till dark. Seems to turn out pretty well. Christian Endeavor meeting tonight. W. Bulman was here tonight."

"Friday, Dec. 3

Fine day but cold. Being threshing wheat all day. Finished at dark. Badly blocked up for room no room to clean the grain. Going to try it tomorrow if all goes well. Oliver Bernard is up with a sow to hog. Got three pigs sick. Perhaps they will die. if so cannot be helped."

"Saturday, 4 December, 1897

Fine day but chilly. Busy cleaning wheat at Mrs. MacKenzie's all day. Cleaned 84 bushels of wheat at twice through the fanners. Came home at dark. Mr. McKinstrie was here this afternoon. Seems pretty smart for a man of his years. Oliver Bernard was after his pig and Rob MacKenzie also. Mr. and Mrs. Darnley Clark were here this evening. Stopt till 11 o'clock. Had a pleasant evening. Invited back to spend an evening in return."

"Sunday, December 5

Dull day. Fall of snow last night. Raining now. Bad roads for church. Sarah Jack is here. Old-fashioned as usual. Pensie not home. On a cruise to the Toombs. Nobody went to church to-day. Snow all gone. Turning cold.'

"Monday, December 6th

Cold day. Hard roads, but not very rough. Cleaned wheat at Mrs. MacKenzie's place. Finished at dinner time. Had 32 bushels to-day and 84 bushels on

Saturday. In fall 31 bushels. Making in all 147 bushels. Our share being 73 1/2 bushels at 80 cts. $58.40 cts. Put away the chaff and put in a loft to carry straw. Albert and Alexander gone to Stanley to the Foresters meeting. Russell going to the Baptist Union. Gilbert going to the office after the mail."

"Tuesday, December 7, 1897

Cold day. Wind northeast. Going to thresh. Had to make a shelter with board to keep the wind off the belt. Threshed the mixed grain. Finished about 3 o'clock and commenced to clean. Worked till dark. There was two she weasels around looking after money to buy Mr. Robertson a fur coat. Artie Macneill fetched our papers tonight and spent the evening. Boys up to Murray Robertson's with a pig."

"Wednesday, Dec. 8

Very fine day. Busy cleaning mixed grain till dinner time. Finished it. Had 92 bushels. My share of it with the seed 7 bushels came to 49 bushels. Commenced to thresh oats after dinner. Mill went wild. Threshed about 35 stooks. There was 2 beggars round. Collecting money for Miss Wise to make a present to her. Bessy was up to get money to pay for the subscription for fur coat."

"Thursday, Dec. 9

Fine mild day. Snowed a little this morning. Busy threshing all day at Mrs. MacKenzie's. About half done the oats. Going to clean tomorrow if all well. The old lady went down to Joseph Gallant to see about some coal. It is $3.50 a ton. He is giving only 26 cts. for oats. Boney Buote has gone west after cattle. The people is going this evening to the Christian Endeavor. There was a man travelling round looking after a factory. George went down to the factory with him."

"Friday, December 10

Soft day. Frost all out of the ground. Busy cleaning oats at Mrs. MacKenzie's all day. Had 152 bushels altogether. It does not seem to turn out very well. Russell gone to Lairds mill with 10 bushels of wheat and 12 bushels of mixed grain to be done by Monday night. Roads is very bad. Got finished after dark. Days very short. Mr. and Mrs. Robertson was here tonight. They are visiting. Mr. Robertson read the 3rd chapter of the 1st epistle of John and prayed. Does not intend to take fur coat."

"Saturday, Dec. 11, 1897

Very fine day. Calm and foggy. Busy threshing all day. Did not finish. About 2 ralleys to thresh. Came home at dark. Had all our work to do. Wood to cut.

Stable to clean. Russell took Gilbert home. Raining hard. Wind backed into the northeast. I hear that A.M. Macneill is very sick with cold and fever. Also that Joseph Macneill of Crapaud is dead. Emily Woolner is a widow again."

"Sunday, December 12

Dull day. Roads very bad. Frost all out with appearance of rain. Preaching in Rustico to-day. Nobody but Mr. Robertson went down. He has to go to Stanley this afternoon. He has a hard road to travel. There was to be meeting in church this evening but do not expect it on account of the weather. Was down at the shore of the old place. Went on to Mosey's old place. He seems to be destroying as much as he can."

"Monday, Dec. 13

Fine day. Ground very soft. Scifts of snow betimes. Finished threshing oats on Mrs. MacKenzie's place. Commenced to clean after that. Finished cleaning at dark. Had 141 bushels all told this time. Moved the thresher and shaker over to Alberts. Going to thresh the next. Have to get some wood for her. Hammond MacKenzie was up with his sow this morning."

"1897, Tuesday, 14th December

Mild day. Went down to Albert's this morning to help him thresh but David Pinneau came to make the granary stair and I came home with him. We made the stair but did not set it up. He is coming back tomorrow if fine. Old Mr. Henry Robertson died to-day at four o'clock, nearly 85 years. So we must all pass away when our time comes."

"Wednesday, December 15

Rainy day with high wind. Ground very sloppy. Busy fixing granary stair and rail. Finished it and hung the outside door. Ren Toombs was here with his big sow. He took her home with him. And Gordon Robertson was here telling about his grandfather. Funeral tomorrow at 2 o'clock. Mrs. George Macneil was here to-day. Russell was over to Laird's mill after flour and mixed grain. Found roads very bad."

"Thursday, December 16

Rainy sloppy day. Roads very bad. Frost all out of the ground. Was up at Mr. Henry Robertson's funeral. He did not seem changed since I last saw him. There was a great many people there considering the state of the roads. George Houston was there with his hearse. The pall bearers walked to the church. They were A.M. Macneill, John Moffat, John Stewart, W.C. Macneill, George and Charles Macneill."

"*Friday, Dec. 17th*

Fine mild day. Boys threshing at Albert's. Finished his wheat tonight. Had Davy Pinneau helping me to fix up the door and granary for winter. Walter Buntain was up here this evening after his pig. He fetched up some potatoes. He says that his father and mother are both sick. Artie Macneill was in here tonight on his way to meeting. Russell went with him."

"*Saturday, Dec. 18*

Very changeable weather. Snowed last night. Soft this morning then snow again. Now the wind is north west and freezing hard. Sent up to Mr. Robertson 841 lbs. of hay. Albert moved up the mill this morning. We threshed two ralleys of wheat this afternoon. Seems to turn out pretty well. Russell took down a load of wood to Mrs. MacKenzie. She was completely out. Gilbert has gone home tonight. He has 7 days of his half month in.

"*Sunday, Dec. 19*

A cold blustery day. Very high wind from the northwest with lots of frost falling. At home all day. Nobody went to church to-day. Roads very rough. Very dull place when there is nobody travelling. Alexander has gone off to the Baptist church tonight. Hope that he may get good."

"*Monday, Dec. 20, 1897*

Fine day but cold. Busy killing pigs to-day. Killed three for ourselves and two for Mrs. MacKenzie. Got done at dark. Had Albert helping us. Going to town tomorrow if all is well. Russell is going to help Oliver Bernard take his pigs into town tomorrow. Going to weigh them now. One weighed 329 and one weighed 279 and one weighed 291 lbs. Mrs. MacKenzie's 324 lbs. and 161 lbs. In all 1385 lbs."

"*Tuesday, Dec. 21st*

Fine day. Alexander gone to town with the pork. I was busy cutting wood for Mrs. MacKenzie all day. Hauled 3 loads out of the woods. Wants to kill her ox tomorrow. Albert gone to the office after the papers. Will Bulman is here. Alexander not home yet. Came home at eleven o'clock. Got paid from Roberts for the mare. Eighty dollars. He got 4 1/2 cts. per lb. for the pork. Russell got a new coat and cloth to make a suit."

"*Wednesday, December 22*

Fine day. Went down to Albert's. Took him down the parcels that came from town and went to Mrs. MacKenzie's with the price of her pork. It came to $21.00 cts. She seems satisfied. If not I can't help it. Came home and commenced to thresh. Finished the turnip land wheat about sundown. Cut up a quarter of beef and salted it. Campbell was here. He has no money and does not want to pay his bill."

"Thursday, 23rd. December
Fine day but cold. In the woods cutting Mrs. MacKenzie's wood. Had Campbell helping me. Got on pretty well. Came home at dark. Cold and tired. Campbell borrowed 10 bags to get chaff at George Macneill's. Gilbert gone to the post for the papers. Got Guardian, Patriot and Montreal Witness. Alexander off to the church to hear the concert. Boys killed an ox for Mrs. MacKenzie. Howard Simpson was here with pig. Did not pay the service fee."

"Friday, December 24
Fine day but cold. Cutting wood in woods. Had Campbell with me. Hard place for wood. Can't make no headway. Will try it another day and then give it up. Got about 20 loads out now. If I had about 10 loads more I would quit it. Gilbert has gone home to spend his Christmas. He got 50 cts. cash and went away happy."

"Saturday, Dec. 25
This is Christmas day. It is fine but cold. Peace on earth Goodwill towards man. The year 1897 will soon be numbered with the past. God has been merciful and kind to me through all the years that are past. We will trust him for the future. I have been home all day doing the chores. Alexander has gone to chop wood for Mrs. MacKenzie. Nettie Robertson was down at 8 o'clock after buttermilk with lantern."

"Sunday, December 26, 1897
Fine day. Preaching in Rustico to-day. Mr. Robertson went down with his new fur coat and sleigh robe. He has been lucky this Christmas time. Mrs. John Robertson died Friday night. To be buried on Tuesday at 2 o'clock. At home all day. Very lonesome. Will Bulman was here. Ren Toombs was here and fetched us some candy, grapes and an orange. He is very kind. Bessy was here on her way to church. Mr. Robertson preached a Christmas sermon and thanked them for his fur coat."

"Monday, December 27
Snow last night but not enough to do any good. In the woods this forenoon cutting wood and hauling out. Came out at 10 o'clock. Russell was up at the mill after Mrs. MacKenzie's flour. Paid Hillman four dollars and forty four cents being the amount of bill furnished. Took up some straw to Mrs. Robert-

son for bedding. MacLeod of Stanley was here with beef to sell. Alexander is off to Glasgow with suit."

"Tuesday, December 28, 1897

Cold day. Some snow fell last night. Drifting. George Macneill and wife was here last night till 11 o'clock. In woods to-day cutting wood. Had Campbell helping me. Cut an oak tree tonight, the last of his race. Mrs. Robertson was buried to-day. Another one has gone to join the grand army. Mort Williams was here to-day with his pig and left her. Boys gone to the Union meeting. They are always gadding about."

"Wednesday, December 29

Very fine day for time of year. Was in the woods taking out Mrs. MacKenzie's wood. Finished at sundown. Lot of work for very little wood. Mort Williams was after his pig. Albert helped him in the sleigh with it. Leon Doucet was round trying to sell boots. Bessy and Letty was here this evening. Letty is very smart. Gave her ten cents for Christmas."

"Thursday, Dec. 30, 1897

Fine day. Cut wood for the boiler. Fed the cattle and got ready to clean wheat. Worked all day. Put it twice through the fanners. Had 65 bushels from 5 bushels sowed which is 13 bushels from one. Not bad. Alex Stewart was here to-day to change $5 into dollar notes. Looks very wild. Alexander is off to Stanley to post some particular letter and pay the shoemaker."

"Friday, December 31st., 1897

Fine mild day. There was a little snow fell to-day. We was down on the road farm cutting boiler wood. Roads are very rough. Mrs. MacKenzie was here this morning to see about getting coal. Leon Goatoue was here after his potatoes. He got 4 bushels. Milton MacKenzie was here looking after his pig. Albert and Bessy was here on their way to the hall. They left Letty home with us. This is the last night of the old year. God has protected us so far."

"January 1, 1898

A soft day. This is New Year's day. I have been at home all day. We have commenced another year but we know not if we shall see the end. God only knows. May He keep us in his care and guide us by His counsel while we are here below and afterwards receive us unto himself. John Toombs was here this morn. Gordon Robertson was here at noon. Boys hauling wood for Mrs. MacKenzie. Russell gone off skylarking."

"Sunday, Jan. 2

A fine day. Very bright. Preaching in Cavendish. Mr. Robertson and Mr. Jackson had service together. They are going to hold their meetings together this week of prayer. There was a good many people in church to-day but they seem very much inclined for horse racing on their way home. It is a poor sign. It shows that they don't mind what they hear."

"Monday, Jan. 3

A fine day. Busy hauling out Mrs. MacKenzie's wood. Finished tonight. This is all that I intend to do for her till she pays me some money. I cut 1 load of wood for myself this forenoon and done the chores this afternoon. Cleaned the stables, cut the wood and fed the cattle. Albert and Bessy and Ma off to the Baptist church. Russell and Alexander off, too."

"Tuesday, Jan. 4, 1898

A very cold day. Heavy frost. Not much doing to-day. Cut wood and cleaned the stables. Albert was up to thresh but found it too cold. Alexander was down at Mrs. MacKenzie's chopping wood. He went to the post-office to get the papers but did not get any. Russell seems to be very uneasy to get off to church but he will not mind what he hears. Our wood is very low."

"January 5, 1898

Fine day after the frost yesterday. Busy threshing Alexander's wheat. Cleaned the stables and cut two loads of wood. Came home and watered the horses and signed 5 checks on the Merchant's Bank in all 53 dollars and 99 cts. The cows did not pair out well this year. No money in anything. Paid Coles and McKay $3.50 cts for horse service. Russell has been down to the New Bridge with coal for Mrs. MacKenzie. Off to the meeting again. Home sometime in the morning. Off his base to-day."

"Thursday, Jan. 6

A very fine day. Very mild. Busy cleaning wheat for Alexander. He had 64 bushels twice through the fanners. Ma and Pensie off to town to spend their milk money. A fool and his money soon part company. There was a man round to-day selling clothes-horses. Wants $1.25 cts for them. Sold him a watch key for 6 cts. Alexander going to the office after the mail. John F. Macneill was in town to-day and bought a fur coat and sleigh robe. His wife got a new set of teeth and if she had a new set of brains she might do for awhile."

"Friday, Jan. 7

Rainy day. Very cold rain. Snow nearly all gone on our road. I went to the woods to-day and cut a load of wood. I was down at Albert's and took him a bottle of codliver oil. He has a bad cough. Oliver Bernard was up to New London. Russell was over at Lairds mill with 15 bushels of mixed grain. Got it home with him. Albert was after coal. Got 900 lbs. No wood home hardly. Bad look-out."

"Saturday, Jan. 8

Fine day. Taking in turnips out of the greenhouse. They kept well but I don't think we will have enough to finish out the fat cattle. Albert was up here this evening. He was not very well. Alexander was over to New Glasgow after his suit of clothes at Ben Stevenson's. Fits pretty well. Pensie off to office after the papers. Russell and Fred Clark off skylarking."

"Sunday, Jan. 9

Very fine day. Alexander and Pensie gone to Rustico church. Was at Ren Toombs for dinner. I was home all day and done up the chores. Russell and Fred off to Rustico. Will Bulman round again. Bessy was in here on her way to meeting. There is to be a big concert at Rustico the last of this month in aid of the Orphan home."

"Monday, Jan. 10

Fine day. Cutting wood on road farm. Cut 12 loads. Mr. Robertson was here saying that he was out of hay. Must take him a load tomorrow. Russell MacLure was here after his pig. Walton Houston was here with his pig. Pierce Macneill and wife was down here this evening. Stayed till 12 o'clock. Heavy white frost tonight. Meeting in Rustico tonight about getting up a concert to get funds for to educate some American children."

"Tuesday, Jan. 11

Cold day. Roads not good. Alexander gone up to the forge to get Maud shod. Russell gone after a load of wood. Pensie gone off to Wedlocks after a present for the wedding party. The boys took up 6813 lbs of hay to Mr. Robertson. Mr. Dickson and Hatty Bulman was here tonight. They postponed their wedding till next Monday. Mrs. MacKenzie was here tonight and Oliver Bernard and his pig."

"Jan. 12, 1898

Dull chilly day. Looks very like a storm. Busy threshing wheat all day. Appears to turn out pretty well. Straw looks like it is going to be scarce. Albert was helping us all day. He expects to kill some of his pigs tomorrow. We will clean if all is well. Oliver Bernard was here today. Will Bulman and Hetty Huston are here tonight. Appears to be some great commotion in New Glasgow."

"Thursday, Jan. 13, 1898

Stormy day. Rained all last night. Busy cleaning wheat today. Had fifty four bushels. Put it in the shop. Going to haul wood tomorrow if I can get a horse shod. Will Bulman and Hetty Houston was here all night. Left for home at daylight. Cleaned wheat all day. Had 55 bushels. Done up the work. Boys off to the Christian Endeavor meeting."

"Friday, Jan. 14

Fine day but cold. Hauling wood from the road farm. Pensie off to Stanley after fixings for dress. There was a man by the name of Meener from Freetown staid here all night. He was trying to sell Hayes Shaker and Cleaner combined. He wanted $40 cash for it. Albert was up at Wedlock's and sold his pork at 5 1/2 cents. He is going to kill on Monday and take them to Breadalbane on Tuesday. He is going to get Pierce to help him kill them."

"Saturday, Jan. 15

A fine day. Roads fairly good. Hauling wood from the road. Ewen MacKenzie got a load of wood under false pretences. Did not pay for it. Mrs. Clift got 3 bushels of oats at 26 cts. Paid for it. Alexander was over at Laird's Mill with twelve bushels of oats to be done on Wednesday. Dan Ross was here collecting for the Stanley Church. I have paid fifteen dollars to that church. Have never been in it yet. Albert and Bessy was up tonight. Ma very sick with her stomach."

"Sunday, Jan. 16

Fine day. There was a fall of snow last night. It may do the roads some good. Pensie and Hetty and Russell gone to church in jaunting sleigh. Too proud to take the box sleigh. 6 P.M. Still snowing. Russell and Pensie and Hetty Houston off to the Baptist church to hear Mr. Jackson preach. It is to be hoped they will hear something to do them good. The text was in Job 9 chapter and 2nd verse. The singing was fine. Mr. Jackson sung the base and Maud played the organ."

"Monday, Jan. 17

Fine day but cold. Boys down helping Albert kill his pork. Had Pensie also. Hetty Houston finished her job of dressmaking and Pensie and Hetty and Alexander and Will Bulman are off to the wedding of Bert Dickson and Hatty Bulman. I was at home all day looking after the cattle and the boiler. It kept me busy doing the chores. Russell is home tonight for a wonder. He seems very uneasy, poor fellow."

"Tuesday, Jan. 18

Fine day but very cold. It is said that it was 20 below zero. I went down and helped Albert to load his pork. It was very cold. Froze my ears coming home. Alexander just home from the big wedding in New Glasgow. The presents were immense. About 120 dollars worth. I was in the woods this afternoon cutting firewood. Got on pretty well. Russell gone to help Albert with pork up to Bradalbane station."

"Wednesday, Jan. 19

Fine day. In woods all day cutting firewood. Came out at dark very tired. Boys at home hauling hay and straw and doing up the chores. Russell gone to New Glasgow to give his measure for a suit of clothes and get the mare shod and fetch home a grist from the mill. James Laird was here to-day wanting wheat at Hunter River for 70 cts. per bushel. Too little."

"Thursday, Jan. 20, 1898

Fine day. In the wood cutting firewood. Albert was helping me after dinner. Boys hauling out. Did not get it all out. Mrs. John Wyand was here and paid her bill for the wheat she got last spring. Six bushels at 80 cts. per bushel $4.80. Albert was up tonight and paid me three dollars on his bill. He was over to New Glasgow, him and Letty and Bessy. They met with an accident. The box came off their sleigh and left them sitting on the snow."

"Friday, Jan. 21st

Stormy day. Wind northeast. Lot of snow falling. Not doing much to-day. Expect it will clear tonight. 6 o'clock. Weather not much better. Did not do much. Cleaned the stables and fed the fat cattle and broke a fork. Not much of a record. Albert paid me three dollars last night. I think I will give him a dollar back to get him a Cardigan jacket to keep him warm for he helps me often."

"Saturday, Jan. 22

Fine day but cold. Murray Robertson was round turning the people out to break the roads for the first time this winter. Snow very hard. I was in the woods cutting wood to-day alone. Boys doing the barn work. Albert was up with a big junk of pork. He was very kind. Ethel MacKenzie was here after somebody to cut her some wood at the door. She has a sore back. Alexander and Pensie and Russell are off to Darnley Clark's on a calie. Artie Macneill fetched the papers."

"Sunday, Jan. 23

Stormy day. Preaching in Rustico to-day. Mr. Robertson went down himself. Wind blowing hard from the southeast. It will likely block up the roads. Poor time now to do anything. Alexander was down at Mrs. MacKenzie's to water the stock. The brook is all drifted up. They can't get any water for the cattle. When it clears up we must try and clear it out. There would be no meeting in the church tonight. If Mr. Robertson got up to Stanley he done well. He has a hard road to travel in the winter time."

"Jan. 24, Monday

Stormy day. Lot of snow has fell. The road will have to be broke. Nothing doing. Out of hay. Want to thresh as soon as we can. Our wood will likely have to wait. 12 o'clock. A.M. Wind backed into the northeast and very cold. Biggest storm of season. Wood to cut, cattle to water and I am not much for work to-day. The storm continued all day and most of the night. It is very cold and rough."

"January 25, Tuesday

Very fine day after the storm. Murray Robertson was round turning out the people to break the roads. They are very bad. The hill is hardly passable. Mr. Robertson and family went down and up. The western gang did not go down. They are a mean set but Murray had better look out or he will be fined. Our mill was nearly covered over. I dug her out and will try and thresh some tomorrow if all is well. Gordon Robertson was down to get his hair cut."

"Wednesday, Jan. 26

Very fine day. Warm and bright. Busy threshing wheat. Finished at sundown. Rats very plenty in it. John Wedlock was here wanting to buy fat sheep for nothing or nearly so. Broke in the yellow mare on the mill. Went well. George Houston was over with the sleigh to Mr. Robertson. Fred Clark was down to Doyle's after a sow that they bought. Expect to move the mill round to the old barn tomorrow."

"Thursday, Jan. 27

Cold day. Moved the mill and fixed up the barn and done up the chores. Albert was up at Pierce's helping to thresh. Murray was there too. Russell went up to the post office after the paper. Had a letter from Rob. He is getting better. He says that David McKay has left for the Island and he is coming to see us and we are to use him kindly for he has been good to him. We will try."

"Friday, Jan. 28

Very cold day. Busy cleaning wheat. Did not get it carried up in granary. Had to take hay to Mr. Robertson. The MacLure boys were up digging a grave in the churchyard today. Mrs. James died yesterday at 3 o'clock P.M. She is to be buried at 1 o'clock Saturday. The boys are off to the division the same as if it was a case of life and death."

"*Saturday, Jan. 29, 1898*
Very cold day. Froze very hard last night. Pump was froze solid. Threshed 2 rallys of mixed grain and done up the chores. Mrs. James Anderson was buried to-day. Oliver Bernard and Lily was here to tea tonight. Put in granary and shop 60 bushels of wheat. Got it all threshed."

"*Sunday, Jan. 30*
Cold day. Preaching in Cavendish to-day. A good many people there to-day. Roads very pitchy. Will Bulman was here to dinner. I did not do any work to-day. Did not feel well at all. Albert and Bessy was here tonight on their way to the Baptist church. They left Letty with us. There was very few there. Church very cold."

"*Monday, Jan. 31*
Cold day. Busy threshing this forenoon and doing up the chores. Walter Houston was up after his pig. He paid 50 cents. Lewie Penowe was up to-day looking after flour. Gave him 25 lbs. He is hard up. Our folk all gone off to the concert at Rustico. Will Bulman was here and says that Mr. Jas. Laird is dead. He had been up to Hunter River about the wheat and was found dead in the horse manger."

"*Tuesday, Feb. 1*
Stormy day. Wind east. Lots of snow fell last night. Murray was out breaking roads this afternoon. The concert came off pretty well at Rustico last night. Did not hear when Jas. Laird will be buried. The turnips are badly frozen. Bad job to have to feed froze turnips to stock. I hear that the proceeds of concert amounted to 20 dollars with prospect of Mr. Toombs giving 5 dollars himself to help in the good cause."

"*Wednesday, Feb. 2*
Fine day. Roads not very good. Busy taking in a stack of hay off Mrs. MacKenzie's place. Had Louis Pinneau helping us. Albert and Bessy was up here to-day on their way to funeral. Alexander and Pensie was over to Jas. Laird's funeral. A great many people there but a lot did not hear of it till over. Mary Laird was here tonight spying round to see what she could see. Boys off to

Baptist meeting. Bad off for something new."

"Thursday, Feb. 3

Fine day. Busy taking in stack of hay off MacKenzie's place. Finished tonight. Was down at Joseph Gallant's after supplies. Roads very bad. Met George Macneill. He had been down at the mill. He says there is great consternation about Laird's property. No will can be found. If so it is likely that everything will be sold before they can straighten the business out. Lawyers will have a pick."

"Friday, Feb. 4

Fine day but cold. Busy cleaning grain in barn all day. Finished in the evening. Had 52 bushels. Took ma down to Ren Toombs after dinner. Did not see anybody. Roads very bad. Seen Bob MacKenzie cutting down his ornamental trees for firewood. Burns magnificent. We had a visit of Louise and Bertha MacKenzie this afternoon. Milton came for them in the evening. They are pretty dry. Boys off as usual tonight. This makes the fifth night this week."

"Saturday, Feb. 5

Fine day. Busy sawing wood. Alexander gone to the mill with some mixing. Did not get it smashed. Fetched home a grist of Albert's. Killed a pig this afternoon. It was very fat. Russell gone to cut some wood for Mrs. MacKenzie. Alexander gone after ma. Mr. Robertson's three little girls were down after buttermilk. Mr. Robertson was down with mission card."

"Sunday, Feb. 6

Rainy morning. Cleared up. After that it snowed. Wind north. Looks very dark. Like snow. Preaching in Rustico to-day. Russell is very uneasy to get away again. He seems to care for nothing but cruising. He will likely be a failure. Preaching in Cavendish."

"Monday, Feb. 7, 1898

Fine day but cold. Commenced to take out the wood. Had some cut ahead. Boys took out eight loads. I was in woods all day alone chopping."

"Tuesday, Feb. 8, 1898

Fine day. Cutting wood all day. They took out 12 loads to-day. Hard work to keep the sleighs going. Wish I had some help."

"Wednesday, Feb. 9

Fine day but very chilly. Cutting wood. Hard work to keep the sleighs going."

"Thursday, Feb. 10

Cold day but clear. Went to the woods to cut wood. Did not expect any help but Campbell came. We got along very well. We will try and take out enough while we are at it and roads good."

"Friday, Feb. 11

Cold day but fine. Weighed 1160 lbs. of hay for Mr. Robertson. This makes 6100 lbs. of hay being the last of the 3 tons I sold him. The price is $24.00."

"Saturday, Feb. 12, 1898

Mild day. Wind south. Looks like a thaw. Going to thresh the rest of Norway oats. Mice eat it nearly all. George Rod, Rustico Road, was here and bought 28 bushels and 28 lbs. of oats at 32 cts. per bushel."

"Sunday, Feb. 13

Fine day after the rain last night. Roads very soft. Preaching in Cavendish to-day. People went walking to church to-day. Only 2 sleighs passed here. Mr. Robertson did not go to Stanley this afternoon. Roads too bad."

"Monday, Feb. 14

Fine day. Froze hard last night. Roads not very good. Busy killing pigs to go to Breadalbane tomorrow. There is 5. They are not as good as they ought to be. Had Campbell cutting wood to-day to clear the piles to be ready to saw. Moved the mill up and set her. I don't know if she is right. Expect to go to Breadalbane station tomorrow."

"Tuesday, Feb. 15

Fine day. Roads not very good. Went up to Wedlocks with the pork. They weighed 897 lbs. at 5 3/4 cts. per lb. and 25 cts. bonus. Left Stanley at 11 o'clock. Got on pretty well till we came to Parson's road. Had very bad roads after that. Had a big hill to climb. Got stuck in the ice and had to get help to get out of Arthur's Hollow. Jim Bob was here sawing and broke his sawing machine. Had to go to Summerside to repair it."

"Wednesday, Feb. 16

Fine day. Not doing much. Got the mare shod. Fixing up the things. Russell hauling out manure. Bessy up here helping them quilt."

"Thursday, Feb. 17

A stormy day. Not doing much. Getting ready to saw. Jim Bob did not come. Campbell was here to-day cutting wood."

"Friday, Feb. 18

Fine day. Cutting wood. Campbell was here after dinner. Jim Bob Stewart came after 2 o'clock. Commenced to saw and finished at dark and moved his saw up to Alex Stewart's. He charged me $2. for his work. Gave Campbell 2 bushels of wheat at 75 cts. per bushel. Settled up with him to date."

"Saturday, Feb. 19

Fine day. At home doing up the work. Alexander gone to Charlottetown after Mrs. MacKenzie's windows. He took her horse and sleigh. He fetched them out after their long wait at Longworth's. He paid her land tax, $2.40. George Rodd, Rustico road, was here to-day. He bought 4 bushels of wheat and 29 bushels of oats. He gave me in all 12 dollars and 25 cts. He got his dinner and Russell drove him up through Cavendish looking after potatoes. He got them at 28 cts.

"Sunday, Feb. 20

Fine day. Preaching in Rustico to-day. Not many went down. Will Bulman was here. He cut his mare badly on the heel. Russell was up to Stanley church. Preaching in Cavendish tonight."

"Monday, Feb. 21

Cold day. High wind. Boys hauling manure to old place. Measured 2 loads of wheat to go to Summerside. George Macniell tells me that he got 80 cts. per bushel cash. R.T. Holman is buying."

"Tuesday, Feb. 22

Cold day. High wind from the east. Went up to Summerside. 2 loads of wheat sold to R.T. Holman. Got 80 cts. per bushel. He paid me the cash for my load. It came to $12.86. Alexander got $13. for his load. Albert had a load up too. I got 90 lbs. of sugar, 5 lbs. of tea, 20 lbs. of beans, 10 lbs. of rice, 5 lbs. of raisins, 1/4 lb. saltpetre, 2 buckets, 1 gallon oil, nails ets. Spent about 9 dollars."

"Wednesday, Feb. 23

Fine day. Busy threshing oats. Badly cut up by mice. Mill goes very well. High wind from the southeast. Did not finish but expect to tomorrow if all is well."

"Thursday, Feb. 24th

Fine mild day. Busy threshing. Finished at dinner time. Will not have many oats. The horses eats it all up. Seems as if we cannot make any headway with oats above anything else. After dinner went over to Hunter River to see Dr. Honeywell about that spot on my nose. He burnt it out. Pretty bad. He says that I have left it too long. Does not give me much encouragement about it. God give me faith to say thy will be done."

"Friday, Feb. 25

Fine day. Had David Pinneau helping me to fix a wood sleigh. Put in 2 bars in wood sleigh and cross bar in shafts. Gave him 1 1/2 bushels of oats for his work. Oliver Bernard was here to-day with his new sleigh. Two bobs and a box. That is like Noah's Ark. It cost 13 dollars. He has swapped his kicking mare and got a McGill mare. She is big but has a blemish. Had her ankle cut with barbed wire."

"Saturday, Feb. 26

Soft snowy day. Boys hauling manure. Russell went to Eddy Toombs boy's funeral. After that to Lorenzo Toombs with the children. They were up getting dresses made. Lelia was up to Albert's to-day. Went up to Murray Robertson's with ma and Lelia. After that with Letty up to James Robert Stewart's. On the go all the time. She has gone for a time. I hope for a long time so we can have some quiet times without so much rush."

"Sunday, Feb. 27

Mild day. Some snow falling. Looks like March weather. Lelia is up here to-day. She did not go to church to-day. She stayed home and cooked the dinner. Alexander did not go to church to-day. He was up at Stanley last night. He got his badge as forester. Very pretty. He is cranky but he will have to be more civil or he will fare worse. Russell and Hetty and Pensie gone to the Baptist church. James Christie died to-day at 9 o'clock aged 55 years. Oliver Bernard came up this morning after Lelia and Mary Gladys."

"Monday, Feb. 28

Fine day. Very mild. Snow by times. Busy hauling manure till 4 o'clock. Russell gone to the mill after a grist and to fetch home some flour for Mrs. MacKenzie. There is a lecture in the hall tonight by Mr. Fullerton. His subject is Mary Queen of Scots. He explained his subject by views of Magic Lantern."

"Tuesday, March 1, 1898

Fine day. Fields covered with snow. Busy hauling out manure all day. Russell and ma gone to James Christie's funeral. He was sick only about a week of inflammation. There was a large funeral. There is a great many people sick now. Dr. Honeywell's wife is very low if not dead by this time. Nelson Orr, wife and family are very sick. Leander Toombs and wife are sick also. Solomon Peter's is lingering a long time."

"Wednesday, March 2

Fine day but roads heavy. Busy cleaning oats all day. Finished it all but the tailings. Had about 118 bushels. Not much for what we sowed. I only sold about 60 bushels out of all we growed. We will have to change our mode of farming and not keep so much stock."

"Thursday, March 3

Fine day. Roads very good. Busy hauling out manure. Alexander up at Bayview House, preparing for the Foresters' great supper. There was a great many people there all bent on having a good time. Some were glad and some were sad and some very idle wild but it is all over now and some think the money spent was better than the supper."

"Friday, March 4

Fine day. Boys hauling out manure all day. Got the most of it out. I was doing up the chores, cleaning stables and feeding cattle, taking in turnips and looking after the fat cattle. Russell is away tonight. He was home last night for a wonder. Albert and Bessy and Letty called in tonight with a boot of Alexander's that Lem Doucet fixed. He says he has no room for it. Russell is put out that he has got no invitation to the Baptist supper. George and John Macneill went down to Cove Head to David Miller's funeral aged 75 years."

"Saturday, March 5

Stormy day. Wind northeast but not cold. Cleaned up some oats this morning and fixed up the cattle. Just resting up on our oars for something to turn up. At 5 P.M. Mr. Robertson came here. He says that Mr. Alexander M. Macneill dropped dead at 4 o'clock. Very sudden. The admonition is be ye also ready for in such an hour as ye think not the son of man cometh. I went down to Albert's to tell him the news. Letty has hurt her face on the lounge. I went up to George Macneill's to tell them. George is not home from Covehead."

"Sunday, March 6, 1898

Very fine day. Preaching in Rustico. Will Laird went down to Rustico and took up W.S. Macneill. There has been a good deal of travelling to-day. Albert is up this evening on his way to church. He says that Letty's face has a bad cut. George Macneill got home tonight from Covehead. The late Alexander Macneill is to be buried on Tuesday at eleven o'clock A.M. The roads are very heavy. It looks like change of weather."

"Monday, March 7

A fine day. Sun very hot. Snow getting soft. Killed a beef to-day. Not very fat.

Robert Wyand was back with his pig again. It is not likely that he will have any pigs. Joe Zebedee Gallant was here to-day. He had been up to Jack Laird's to hire. He says that he is going to work there all summer at $6 a month. Boys hauling home hay. It takes a lot to do us."

"Tuesday, March 8, 1898

Fine day. Roads pretty good. Mr. Alexander Macneill was buried to-day. A great many people at the funeral. He was in his 78th year. All have to go. He left the farm to John Franklin and his money in the bank and stock to his wife. So John Franklin and Campbell says. Oliver Bernard and Lelia was here after the funeral. Mrs. MacKenzie and 2 children was up here this afternoon. She wanted her bill. It was $12.50 cts. John Campbell and Mr. MacLeod was here looking after seed wheat. They wanted 25 bushels. They took a sample. David Laird lectured in the hall tonight."

"Wednesday, March 9

Fine day. Hauling out manure in the forenoon. Took up a load of hay in afternoon. Boiled the boiler and done up the chores. Going to feed the fat cattle and empty the boiler. Boys off to Laird's sale. Russell looks like as if he would cook himself he is in such a fluster to get off to the supper at Bay View house. He got a bag.

Boys home from the sale. They seem disappointed. Did not buy anything. Alexander gone to the Baptist supper. Pensie off to the concert at New Glasgow. They ought to settle down soon."

"Thursday, March 10

Fine day. Very mild. Roads very soft. A great many pilgrims travelling round. Alfred Macneill was round to-day. Mr. and Mrs. Robertson and family were round this evening. I was not at the Baptist social and supper. They made about $32. Not so bad at all. There was a concert and pie social at New Glasgow hall the same night. I did not hear how much they realized. There was a funeral at New Glasgow of the late Mr. Smith aged 24. Pensie came home tonight. Boys been hauling manure on Mrs. MacKenzie's place."

"Friday, March 11

Fine soft day. Looks like spring. I am home doing the barn work. Boys hauling manure on Mrs. MacKenzie's place. Ma has gone down on a caly to Aunt Bell's. Has a fine day for the race. There is a lot of water on the road. Russell is going after ma. She has put in a good half day talking. She will be sick. Boys gone off to the Divison. Very zealouse. Mr. Robertson's children was here last night. They had a hard time getting through the water after their buttermilk."

"March, Saturday 12

Fine day but roads very bad. Fields nearly bare. John Campbell and Mr. Howat was here this morning after wheat. They gotten bushels at 75 cts. per bushel. Russell drove Hetty down to Mrs. MacKenzie's this morning. Went to the woods after dinner to cut logs to make a stable floor for the old horse-stable. Got flour and other logs proved unsound. Snow in the woods is very treacherous. Albert fetched up Hetty Houston this evening and waited for his mail. He has been sick with the hickups all day."

"Sunday, March 13

Very soft day. Snow nearly all gone. Roads very bad. Not many in church to-day. Our people walked there to-day. George Simpson is to take Mr. Robertson up to Stanley this afternoon. Alexander is off on a visit to his friends. Russell has gone off to the Baptist church this evening with Pensie and Hetty Houston."

"Monday, March 14

Soft day. Snow nearly all gone. Roads very bad. Alexander drove Hetty Houston to John Fraser's. She did not stop there. The little girl is very sick. They are after the doctor this morning. They drove her home to Glasgow. We were busy splitting wood all day. Mr. Robertson came down this evening. He got Russell to drive him down to Toombs after his butter. Ham was busy smashing grain for Ren Toombs."

"Tuesday, March 15

Very fine day. Froze hard last night. Went down and helped Albert to take in his stock of oats and threshed it. Had Leonard Meeks and Demos Gallant helping him. Finished at 4 o'clock. Boys hauled home 2 jags of hay. Want to take in a stack of hay as soon as possible. George Macneill had a crowd cutting poles. Artie was over after an axe."

"Wednesday, March 16

This is St. Patric day in the morning. It opened fairly fine but commenced to snow at dinner time very thick. We were cutting poles this forenoon. Had Demos with me. He went with Albert this afternoon."

"Thursday, Mar. 17

Fine day. Busy cutting poles. Cut half a day. Demos went down to Albert's to work at sleigh. Boys not pulling well."

"Friday, Mar. 18

Very fine day. Busy cutting poles. Had Demos helping me. Cut hard all day.

Came out of woods at dark. Very tired. Not so smart as I used to be. Boys been hauling logs up to Stanley. They went up from Bay View on ice. Came by the ponds."

"Saturday, Mar. 19

Fine day. Busy cutting poles to-day until dinner time on our own place. After dinner on Mrs. MacKenzie's place. Ma gone down to Ren Toombs again. Seems to be something wrong down there. There is a deputation of New Glasgow girls gone down to Alberts'. Laura Houston and Jennie Stevenson. Business affairs of state."

"Sunday, March 20

Fine day. Roads very sloppy. Snow last night nearly all gone. Russell gone to drive Mr. Robertson down to Rustico church. Alexander gone somewhere. Ma gone to stay at Ren Toombs. Tillie Clark and her sister gone to Rustico church. Russell has gone to Stanley to drive Mr. Robertson. He had his driver there. Me and Pensie done up the work. Laura Houston and Jenny Stevenson was here tonight and Bessy. May Hooper is on the track. We will likely have another bawl soon."

"Monday, Mar. 21

Fine day. Very high wind from the west. Froze hard last night. Busy cutting poles on Mrs. MacKenzie's place. Very poor place to cut poles. Bad road at the edge of the woods. Water up to the horse's belly."

"Tuesday, Mar. 22

Fine day. Busy cutting poles. Had nobody to help me. Demos Gallant has not come. He promised to help me. Alexander took up a log up to the mill this morning. He fetched home a load of plank. Mr. Robertson was down here to-day looking after hay, straw and turnips. Sent him up 425 lbs. of hay. Arty Macneill was here tonight on his way to the prayer-meeting at the manse."

"Wednesday, Mar. 23

Squally day with rain. I was in the woods to-day making roads and taking out poles. Was in at Albert's this morning with a letter and the paper. He is not very well this spring. Alexander took up a log to the mill and fetched home a load of plank by the sea ice. Russell was hauling poles this forenoon. Bessy was up this evening after the mat frames. The hooking craze is on now pretty bad."

"Thursday, March 24

Cold windy day. Busy cutting poles on MacKenzie place. Had Demos Gallant with me. Russell is hauling out. Road very rough. Milton MacKenzie came into the woods. He does not seem to have much to do. He says that Bob has gone to town with 18 bushels of wheat. He is going to fetch home some wire with him. Alexander went down to Toombs after his mixed grain. He is pleased with his returns. Roads very bad."

"Friday, Mar. 25

Very fine day. In woods cutting poles on home place. Cut a good many. I think that we have enough for this year. Had Demos Gallant helping me. A Mr. MacInnis of Glasgow road was here to-day after wheat. He got six bushel at 80 cts. per bushel. Lucy Gallant was here after hen feed. Left a bag to put half bushel in. Gordon Robertson was here tonight. Him and Russell are off to the Division. Ma not home yet. She ought to stay altogether with the Toombs.

"Saturday, March 26

Fine day. Roads very rough. Froze hard last night. I went up to Stanley to-day after a pair of shoes for myself and Pensie. They cost $3.50. Nails and spikes 55 cts. Mr. Robertson's children was down this evening after eggs. Got 3 dozen. No mail tonight. Something wrong with the state of Denmark."

"Sunday, Mar. 27

Fine day. Preaching in Cavendish to-day. Roads very bare. Oliver Bernard called in here this morning on his way to church. Walter Buntain and Maria were also. They came home to dinner and went to the Baptist church in the evening. Bob McKenzie was here also. Russell drove Mr. Roberston up to Stanley this afternoon. They went by they sea ice and then up the bay to Stanley.

"Monday, March 28

Fine day. Down on the raod farm cutting poles. Done very well. It was a pretty good place to cut poles. Lelia came past while we were cutting on her way to Ren Toombs. He is killing pigs for town. Minnie is not very well. Ma not home yet. She can stay altogether if she likes. Bernard wants to buy the farm on the road. I think that I will sell it.

"Tuesday, March 29

Fine day. Busy fixing up the pig house in fornoon. David Penowe's wife and daughter was here to dinner. Demos Gallant came after dinner. We commenced to pull down the old House. It is hard to down. It is put together with 4 in nails. Got the roof off but not the logs. A lot of stuff in the old buildings.

"Wednesday, Mar. 30

Fine day. Busy pulling down the old house. Took the logs down and commenced to take the chimney down. Lots of stone of very good quality. It is very hard work handling them. It makes a lot of rubbish, these old houses. I wish the job was done. The ground is so very soft and mushy it makes it hard to move around."

"Thursday, Mar. 31
Dull day. Looks like snow or rain. Busy putting sills under the old house. Very nasty job. So much mud and so much heavy lifting. I wish it was up at its place so we would be done with it. It is going to cost more than it will be worth when it is on the spot. Had to give up work at 3 o'clock on account of the snow and rain."

"Friday, April 1
Dull day. Raining this morning. Not doing much this forenoon. Demos Gallant gone down to Albert's to fix a wood sleigh. Boys started the boiler in afternoon. Working at old house. Put runners under it and getting ready to haul. Ground very wet and sloppy. If it does not freeze we cannot haul the house."

"Saturday, April 2
Fine morning. Froze hard last night. Commenced to haul the old house this morning. Getting along fine till about ten o'clock when we broke the shaft of stumping machine which delayed us for 2 hours till we made a new one. Got it fixed and started after dinner. Got on well. Did not get it to the place that we wanted it. Will settle it soon. Demos went home tonight. He put in three days this week at 55 cts. per day."

"Sunday, April 3
Fine day. Wind southeast. Very chilly. Feels like rain or snow. Mr. Robertson went down to Rustico this morning. Russell disappointed him in not going to drive him to church. He got Bob MacKenzie to pilot him down. Russell has gone to take him up to Stanley this afternoon. Mrs. MacKenzie is sick. Pensie has gone down to see her. George Macneill visits her often to minister to her spiritual and temporal wants. He is a good Samaritan I suppose."

"Monday, April 4
Fine day. Finished moving the old house. Made a good job of it. Moved the mill down at dinner. Set her and commenced to thresh. Got on pretty well. Took home a load of hay. Sent home Mosey's wire. Mary Penowe was up here to-day. Helda MacKenzie was up to change eggs. Russell is off to the Baptist Union. Alexander is gone to the forge after nails to shoe Albert's mare. Pensie

was down helping Bessy to hook her mat. Demos has not come home yet."

"Tuesday, April 5

Fine day but cold. Busy threshing down at the old barn. Finished threshing at 4 o'clock. Commenced to clean. Turning out well I think. Alexander took up 350 lbs. of hay to Mr. Robertson. Roads very bad. I will not let him have any more. He will have to look somewhere else for his hay after this."

"Wednesday, April 6

Dark cold day. Busy cleaning oats all day till 3 o'clock. After that put in the mill and moved the old house about 10 feet nearer the barn. Russell hauled three loads of hay and harrowed the lane. After tea we fixed the lane for hauling. William A. Houston went up on Sulky to Stanley to the lodge. Albert was in here tonight. He had been in on the Cavendish Road after a man to help him saw wood. Dodo promised him to come. Milton MacKenzie was here tonight."

"Thursday, April 7

Dull day. Snowed some last night but not enough to do any good. Russell has gone to haul longers on Mrs. MacKenzie's place. I am at home not doing much. Got a very sore knee. It don't care about working to-day. Ren Toombs was here to-day. He came back to the old barn and fetched me a bottle of brandy. He is very kind. I do not deserve such kindness for I have not done anything for them. Russell and Albert took Gordon Robertson over to New Glasgow to put him through the Division. He was not black beaned this time."

"Friday, April 8

Blustery day. Some snow falling to-day. Not much can be done in weather like this. It being Good Friday, the wind is northwest. Demos Gallant went home. I fixed up the yard and done up the chores. There was a great square-up at the Division tonight. Big Bear is on the rampage about Gordon Robertson going into the Division but he may snap his teeth. Who cares."

"Saturday, April 9

Fine day. Alexander gone to Stanley with logs to saw for studding in afternoon. Busy fencing on Mrs. MacKenzie's place to keep the cattle off the grass land. Frost not out at all. Artie Macneill fetched the papers. There seems every probability of war between Spain and the United States. May God scatter the nations that delight in war."

"Sunday, April 10

Fine day but cold. Preaching in Cavendish to-day. Not many there. Russell took a waggon. Ma went up to church but did not mind the text. Poor memory indeed. Bob MacKenzie drove the minister up to Stanley. He is so nervous that he can't drive his own horse. Roads are very bad and no better."

"Monday, April 11

A fine day. Froze hard last night. Busy cleaning wheat with separator. Separated 370 bushels of White Chaff. Alexander was up at Stanley after his studding. He got 21 lbs. of wire. James McKinstrie was here to dinner. He looks as if his time is short. There was a peddling horse doctor going round this afternoon. He does not give his name. Margaret Macneill was here this evening after a rooster. Mrs. George Macneill was here this evening. Boys gone to Union meeting."

"Tuesday, April 12

A very fine day. Froze hard last night. I was busy sharpening pickets at the road at the old place. Did not finish them but will finish them in the morning if all goes well. Mr. Robertson and wife went down this afternoon going to Rustico. Mirtle Macneill was here after eggs. Bessy and Letty was up this evening. The mail has arrived. The war scare between Spain and the United States is not so bright as last week. Perhaps it may settle down without blows. We hope it may be so."

"Wednesday, April 13

Fine day. Finished sharpening pickets. Alexander has gone down to Rustico with team after lumber. He fetched six dollars and 30 cts. worth. It costs quite a lot to build. He will know something about it by the time that he builds as much as I have done. I was in the woods this afternoon burning brush. It burnt well. It clears off fine and there is not much danger of fire. Milton MacKenzie was in with me. Cannot fence yet. Albert ploughed his road up to back field."

"Thursday, April 14

Rainy day. Commenced to rain last night. It will do good and draw the frost out of the ground and start the grass. We made a set of swingle trees this forenoon getting ready for planting."

"Friday, April 15

Cloudy day. Sloppy weather. Very backward for time of year. Hauling straw and hay from the old barn. Hard time on fodder. Sawed blocks for dyke. Could not put up the fence on account of the frost. Our work is very much behind."

"Saturday, April 10

Fine day but very foggy. Begins to look like rain. Getting cold. Roads very bad. Do not dry up. Frost not coming out much. Raining hard this evening. Demos Gallant started for home but did not go any further than Robertson's. He turned and came back and stayed all night. The mail arrived. It looks like war between Spain and United States."

"Sunday, April 17

Fine day. High westerly wind. It will dry up the roads if it continues. Preaching in Rustico this morning. Mr. Robertson went down himself. Horse goes well. Oliver and Lelia was up here this afternoon. They had Nell in the buck board. Went home before preaching. Bessy came up to go to church. She took sick and had to be driven home. Will Bulman was here also."

"Monday, April 18

Fine day. Froze last night. Alexander went down to Rattenbury's after shingles and boards. I lent him five dollars cash. We were putting out manure, cleaning up the yard. Russell went to the mill with 8 bushels of wheat. White Fyfe. I hope the flour will be better than the White chaff."

"Tuesday, April 19

Fine day. Busy putting out manure. Had Zebedee helping me. Cleaned up the yard and hauled some hay. I done up the chores. Ma and Pensie went up to Stanley with eggs. She got a lot of things. Room paper and lots of things. Laura MacKenzie was up after bags to haul oats to Rustico down to Moffat's vessel."

"Wednesday, April 20

Fine day. Busy fencing. Zebedee Gallant going to plant trees. Gone down to dig them on the road farm. Frost not out. Did not succeed in planting many. Fixed the dulse road. Russell hauled 51 bushels and 28 lbs. of oats down to vessel for Mrs. MacKenzie. Went up to mill after that with grist of wheat. Fetched home ours. Had 285 lbs. of flour from 8 bushels of White Fyfe about 37 lbs. to bushel."

"Thursday, April 21

Very rainy day. Busy killing pigs for town. Do not know when we will get them in. Roads very bad. The pigs look very well but they are small. It does not pay to feed pigs in the winter time."

"Friday, April 22

Fine day. Busy fencing all day. Alexander gone to town with the pigs. He took a span of horses. The roads were very bad. He got home at 9 o'clock. He got 6

1/2 cts. per lb. for his pork and 25 bonus. He fetched two barrels of corn meal. It cost $2.25 per bbl. Albert and Bessy and Pensie went to Maud Bryenton's funeral. She died of consumption aged 19 years. Artemas Macneill was in here on his way to Davy Jack's with a pair of boots to be repaired."

"Saturday, April 23

Fine day but cold. High wind from the west. Busy fencing all day. Prosper Blacquiere's boys round selling fresh herring at 10 cts. per dozen. Taras Doiron around looking after a horse to buy. Bob Roberts was around buying sheep. He bought 3 at $5 each. In all 15 dollars. Mosey Gallant was here wanting to buy the farm on the road. I asked 350 dollars for it. Mary Penowe was up with clams. William S. Macneill was here to tea tonight."

"Sunday, April 24

Fine day but cold. Preaching in Cavendish to-day. Ren Toombs was here and put his big horse in stable and went to church. He came back and had dinner with us. Maggy Clark and Hetty Houston came home from church. They did not go to church this evening on account of rain. It commenced to rain at dark and poured all night long."

"Monday, April 25

Cold disagreeable day. Showers of rain with cold driving wind from northeast. Alexander has been down to Winsloe road with Bob Roberts with 4 sheep. Ren did not go to Roberts with his. William Moffat was round looking after Potatoes and Oats to fill up the vessel. He says that he heard that war had been declared and fighting begun. Russell gone off with Hetty and Maggy Clark to take them home."

"Tuesday, April 26

Cold blustery day. Snowed last night. Very cold and blustery. Hard time on cattle and sheep. Fred Clark and Russell got astray last night. War has commenced between Spain and the United States. Been cold and windy all day with no sign of abating. This is two days of storm with no prospect of clearing up. There is a heavy sea on. There will likely be dulse when the storm moderates."

"Wednesday, April 27

Cold and windy. Roads very bad. Boys down on the road farm hauling poles to make a line fence between MacKenzie and I. Albert and I went to Stanley after peas and clover seed. We bought 12 bushels of peas and 114 lbs. of clover seed. The peas cost $1.50 per bushel and the clover cost 84 cts. for Late

Vermont and 9 for Alsyke and 15 cts. for White clover. Pierce Macneill drove me down from Stanley and stayed till 10 o'clock."

"Thursday, April 28

Fairly fine. Busy fencing below the road. Russell put up a good fence across the farm. Russell hauled a good many poles from the old place. The boys hauled straw and hay from the old barn. There is lots of ice back on the shore. Philissy Doucet found the foreyard with truss and gear attached. Joseph Gallant was here to buy the road farm. Price 350 dollars. He can't get it till the fall if then."

"Friday, April 29

Cold rainy disagreeable day. Not doing much. Fixed the wire in the lane. Going to fix the line fence back of the pig house. Hard time on cattle. Feed going away very fast. Perhaps the grass may grow soon if it turns warm. I put in gate post in the cow lane. Did not finish it. Expect to do it tomorrow. Milton MacKenzie went past with a glass jar looking after milk. Alexander has taken Johnny and gone down to Ren Toombs to see if he is going to Charlottetown. He wants to send after his watch at Wellner's."

"Saturday, April 30

Very rainy day. Wind southeast. Rained most of last night. Lots of ice on the shore. The fishermen had to take in their back lines to save them. Very backward for farming. I fixed the dyke by the road with stone and sods. Went down to the shore. There is lots of ice along the coast yet. Russell has gone down to Rustico after wire for fencing. He had to go to Frank Andrew's after it. He got 25 lbs. at 2 1/4 cts. per lb. 56 cts. He got 2 springs also."

"Sunday, May 1

Fine day but cold and foggy. We have had a long spell of backward weather. Preaching in Rustico to-day. Ma and Alexander have gone down to Ren Toombs to get their tea and hear the news and see Old Bell and to know if she takes her medicine and if she wears her white handkerchief round her head. Ma has got home. Ren is not going to town tomorrow with his cattle."

"Monday, May 2

Cold day. Wind north. Ice on shore. Rain this forenoon. Got stuff to make a gate. This morning was fencing on the cape at the old place all day. George Macneill took his 2 fat cattle to Bob Robert's and a load of wheat also. Had a calf cast last night and a lamb to-day. Boys off to Baptist Union tonight."

"Tuesday, May 3

Fine day. Down on road farm to-day. Fencing on line. Put up a good fence round our share. MacKenzie's have not put their share of fence yet. Pensie came down after me. There was a Mr. Cameron of New London came after 14 bushels of wheat for Mr. Howat. Went down to the road after that. Minnie came through the woods with our tea. She is very kind. Finished at sundown. Came home. Campbell was around looking after hay, straw, oats and flour. Did not give him any."

"*Wednesday, May 4*

Fine day. Busy fencing on shore bank of old place. Put up the line fence by Albert's after tea. Got a stick to make gate posts from Philissy Doucet. Price 50 cts. Paid in cash. He got 100 lbs. of flour on credit. Price 3.00. Put line fence between Mrs. MacKenzie's. Very rotten longers."

"*Thursday, May 5*

Fine day. I am fencing still. Came home at 10 o'clock. Fixed up the chores till dinner time. At dinner there was a man of the name of Ford here looking after wheat. He only offered 85 cts. per bushel. Did not sell any at that price. Mr. Robert Johnson got 5 bushels White Chaff wheat at 90 cts. per bushel. Maxim Peter's got 12 1/2 bushels of White Chaff wheat at 90 cts. per bushel. Paid cash $3.50."

"*Friday, May 6*

Fine day. Looks like rain. Ice in night. Vessels in the ice. Fixed the dulse road this morning. Road machine expected. Did not come. I went down to Rusticoville to MacCoubrey's after harness. Had to wait till he done it. Cost 35 cts. Russell's cost 25 cts. In all 60 cts. Domini Buote for shoe 4 cts. To Joe Gallant for bottle of oil $1.00."

"*Saturday, May 7*

Fine day. But cold. Ice back on shore. Nothing done in planting yet. The road machine is at work to-day in this district. Road supervisor very sick. Parkman here to dinner. Started the plough this afternoon. Did not finish the piece. Pensie and Bessy gone to Stanley to Wedlock's with eggs. I was fencing on the line back. Field poles very rotten. Did not finish it."

"*Sunday, May 8*

Fine day but cold. Ice all back on shore. Very poor prospects of spring. Hay getting low. Oats short. At home alone. Our people all gone to church. Lelia and Laura and Oliver and Ren Toombs was here to dinner. Very cold for young lambs tonight. Boys off to the Baptist Church tonight. I have just heard that

Silas Smith of Washington Territory died very suddenly at his uncle Ewan MacMillan's West River. He is to be buried tomorrow from J.D. Smith's."

"Monday, May 9

Fine day but cold. Ice on shore. Very high tide. We commenced to plough the road farm to-day. It is pretty dry. We must hurry up with our work. It is getting late and our hay is very low. We have a lot of work to do. Met John MacLure Soldier. He says that he is not called to the States yet."

"Tuesday, May 10

Very cold. Froze hard last night. Boys down ploughing on road farm. I am at home doing the work. I fetched up a little jag of hay. Did not like to fetch much."

"Wednesday, May 11

Fine day. Boys ploughing on the road farm. They will finish to-day. I was up at Montana fixing the fence to keep the cattle out. The fence is very near past repairing. Alexander went to Stanley after 2 bags of pease. 1 bag cost 2.40 and the other cost 2 dollars at Archie MacLeod's. Albert got that one. He bought this spring 6 bushels of pease. I bought 2 bushels of pease."

"Thursday, May 12

Very fine. It is nearly hot enough for summer. We are busy sowing the road farm to-day. I sowed 11 bushels of pease and 6 bushels of Norway oats. Albert sowed the most of his by hand. I carted off the stones that was on the upper field."

"Friday, May 13

Fine day. Down on the road farm. Rolling. Ground very dry. Dust flying. Albert was late getting down. He struck oil this morning. He got 4 seal skins one as big as a cow."

"Saturday, May 14

Rainy day. Nothing doing on the land to-day. Working at seal skins. There was a good lot of fat on the skin that Albert gave me. Ma went down this morning to see the seals. Tom Doyle's horse was here this afternoon. Mr. Ramsay was here with Dufferin. Oliver Bernard was up with his sow."

"Sunday, May 15

Fine day. Preaching in Rustico to-day. Minnie and baby and Ren was up this afternoon. Will Bulman and Horace Ling was here this afternoon. Meeting in church tonight. Good many gone up."

"Monday, May 16

Fine day. Sowed 6 1/4 bushels of wheat on Mrs. MacKenzie's place and 1 bushel of hay seed and 12 lbs. of clover seed. She went down to the ferry. She got it at Brad Lepage's. It cost $2.20 per bushel. She gave me five dollars to pay for her share of seed. I sowed 2 bushels on our place. Milton MacKenzie bought a pig for 1.50. There was a lamb died last night."

"Tuesday, May 17

Rainy day. Nothing doing on the land this forenoon. Separated 12 bushels of wheat this forenoon. Put out manure after that. Russell gone after Campbell to help us. Wedlock was here after cattle. Will call again."

"Wednesday, May 18

Pretty fine day. Busy putting out manure for potatoes all day. Had Campbell helping us. Put out a good lot. Manure very much heated. Our potatoes are likely to be short this spring. Straw and hay both low. Hard spring on man and beast."

"Thursday, May 19

Fine day. Busy putting out manure. Long road to haul. Had truck wagon and 2 carts. We stopped at dinner. Campbell commenced to spread manure after dinner. The rest of us went to sow oats on Mrs. MacKenzie's place. I sowed 26 bushels this afternoon but did not finish the field. I measured up 21 bushels of oats at Mrs. Mac's granary. Oliver Bernard and his three children were up here this evening. He took a load of wheat up to the mill. Got some oats here on the way home."

"Friday, May 20

Rainy day. Went down to field and worked a while but had to give up. We came home and stayed till after dinner. Ham Binns was round selling codfish. They were very large. Albert was up to get his hair cut. Donald Simpson was down with his sow to hog. Let Campbell have 5 bushels of wheat. Boys harrowing. Very wet."

"Saturday, May 21

Fine day. Busy sowing wheat on Mrs. MacKenzie's place. Sowed 8 bushels of wheat and 4 bushels of oats and also sowed 3 pecks hayseed and 12 lbs. of clover seed. I also sowed 1 bushel of hayseed on the potato land and 10 lbs. clover in all, 13 bushels of hay seed, 22 lbs. of clover seed at 9 cts. per lb. $1.98

cts. I have sowed to date 44 bushels of oats and 146 bushels of wheat on home place. 2 bushels White Chaff."

"Sunday, May 22

Fine day but cold. Preaching in Cavendish to-day. Did not see many going. Mr. Secord was round yesterday selling books for the Bible Society. We got a nice book from him. Demos was round buying grain for seed. Our folks was at preaching to-day. Does not appear to have done then any good. They are preparing to go to the Baptist church this evening. Always on the tramp. May they find the Pearl of Great Price. O Lord, grant us Thy blessing. Guide us by Thy blessing. Guide us by Thy counsel. Amen."

"Monday, May 23

Fine day. Busy at work on MacKenzie place planting potatoes."

"Tuesday, May 24

Fine day. Busy putting out manure for potatoes on Mrs. MacKenzie's place. Had Campbell helping me. Wheatley came and bought the fat cattle for 67 dollars and fifty cents. I went down to Oliver Bernards after 5 bushels of White Fyfe wheat. Cost $4.50. Sold 9 bushels of wheat to Toph Penowe for 1 dollar per bushel."

"Wednesday, May 25

Fine day. Sowed 7 bushels of White Chaff wheat on home farm. Hammond MacKenzie was up with his sow. Hope he will pay and not be mean. It costs to keep these hogs up. Came home and commenced on the field by the barn.

"Thursday, May 26

Fine day. Busy sowing potato land wheat. Sowed 13 bushels on turnip land and potato land and sowed the grass seed after that. Russell and Albert went to town with the cattle. Had trouble with Stanley cattle. No driver with them. Wheatley mean."

"Friday, May 27

Fine day. Busy harrowing the wheat land. After dinner sowed the sod land on old place. Sowed 21 bushels of oats. It appears to harrow well. I am very tired tonight. Too much travelling between the places. We are getting along with planting pretty well."

"Saturday, May 28

Cloudy with showers of rain. Sowed mixed grain on Mrs. MacKenzie's place on the field that potatoes is planted in. Did not sow it down. May manure it this fall if they like. After dinner sowed the field by house with mixed grain. Do not expect much. Fetched up a jag of hay and done up the chores."

"Sunday, May 29

Fine day. Preaching in Rustico to-day. Mr. Sutherland of Zion church is exchanging pulpits with Mr. Robertson. Russell is driving Mr. Sutherland down with Mr. Robertson's horse and wagon. Ma is very sick with the cold."

"Monday, May 30

Cloudy day. Very dull weather. Wind east. Sowed the field by old barn. Sowed 4 1/2 bushels of White Chaff wheat on west side. Left over an acre for potatoes on the east side. Sowed mixed grain and barley down by old house. I went over to New Glasgow to Frank Andrews. Got 10 lbs. of clover seed at 9 cts. per lb. also 103 lbs. of barbed wire at 2 1/2 cts."

"Tuesday, May 31

Fine day. It rained hard last night. Commenced to plough the pasture field above the house. Alexander and Russell commenced in the morning. Albert came up after dinner. Got on well. I sowed the grass seed on piece by old house."

"Wednesday, June 1

Fine day. Busy ploughing with three ploughs on field above the house. I was ploughing myself. Find that I have not forgot the way yet. Took first prize for ploughing west ridge. The team goes very rash. Maud will never be better and the yellow mare is no better but we have to take things as we find them for no better and much worse."

"Tuesday, June 2

Fine day. Boys went down to finish harrowing the field on old place. They finished by dinner time and came home. I was ploughing all day. Alexander ploughed after dinner. Russell commenced to harrow the field after dinner. Turned cold. Wind east. Sheep's pasture is getting small."

"Friday, June 3

Fine day but cold. Wind east. Alexander ploughing head lands. I cleaned 28 bushels of Norway oats and commenced to sow after dinner. Sowed till sundown. Did not finish. Expect tomorrow if all is well. Albert is planting his potatoes to-day. Letty was up all day. Joe came after her."

"Saturday, June 4

Fine day for working but cloudy. Finished sowing the field this morning and sowed some peas and mixed feed for the pigs after dinner. Put out 9 loads of manure for mangels. Seems as I will never get them planted. Alexander has left his work and gone on a mission to the American Jews. Came home very late. Sleepy all day."

"Sunday, June 5

Fine day. Cleared up bright. Preaching in Cavendish to-day. Russell is gone to the Baptist church and likely to Pierce Macneill's to dinner. Alexander is putting in a day sleeping. Hetty Houston is here to dinner to-day. Sheep are on the rampage to-day. Albert was over at New Glasgow to-day. Mr. Robertson preached for Mr. Jackson to-day. There is going to be a big time at the Baptist church this week."

"Monday, June 6

Dull foggy day. Heavy mist falling this morning. Campbell was round this morning looking after grub and seed oats. Very hard times for a poor man. I ploughed the little field and harrowed it this forenoon. I am going to plough the turnip land this afternoon if all is well. I ploughed all the afternoon. Got on well. The land is pretty mellow."

"Tuesday, June 7

Fine day. I was ploughing the turnip land all day till tea time. Finished. Then came home. Did not roll the wheat land. We had no hay for the horses. I put in a gate post, cleaned the stables and pumped water for the cows. Russell was rolling the wheat land on Mrs. MacKenzie's place. Alexander is planting potatoes on the old place. Aunt Bell is off to town to-day to get gears. Johnny Big Eyes went down with a thing that he calls a trotter."

"Wednesday, June 8

Rainy morning. Cleared up at 7 o'clock. Put up a fence on Mrs. MacKenzie's place. I supplied the material. The wire cost $2.57, staples 10 cts. Came home went and got the mare shod. Russell went up to Mark's factory with lobsters for Joe Doucet. Pensie and Bessy off to Stanley with eggs."

"Thursday, June 9

Fine day. Busy rolling the wheat land. Finished at 2 o'clock and commenced to roll the oat land. Did not finish it. Ma and Pensie gone down to see Mrs. Bulman. She is very sick with inflammation of lungs. Mrs. Murray Robertson was down here this evening. Joe Doucet was up with a check on Merchants

Bank of Halifax with nobody's name to it. No good."

"Friday, June 10

Cold day. High northwest wind. Fishermen going to catch fits. Their traps are close in shore. Will break up with the sea. We are busy putting out manure for our turnips. Have Campbell helping me. It is a long piece to haul the manure. Albert's boy and horse helping us after tea. Alexander drilling the turnip ground. The boys are not likely to make good farmers. Too much hurry sometimes."

"Saturday, June 11

Fine day. Busy putting out manure for turnips. Had Campbell helping me. He worked well all day. It is too far to have manure for turnips. It will take us all day Monday to finish hauling manure. Fixed the fence to keep the young cattle in their pasture. Mrs. MacKenzie is on the rampage about her pastures. She keeps too much stock."

"Sunday, June 12

Cloudy day. Preaching in Rustico to-day. 2 waggons of Jack Franklins went down to church to-day to see what they can see. Alexander and Pensie gone off on a mission in Rustico on the pretence of hearing how Mrs. Bulman is. They took my horse and waggon. It is pretty grand. Ben Stevenson, wife and family have made a raid on Albert. Poor fellow."

"Monday, June 13

Fine day. Had Campbell helping to put out manure. Finished at 3 o'clock. Then commenced to spread. We done six rows and Alexander commenced to drill. Boys off to the Union prayer meeting"

"Tuesday, June 14

Fine day. Pensie gone after the Jacks to shear the sheep. We got our sheep out of the woods. They look fine. They have pretty good fleeces. I paid Jacks 88 cts. cash for shearing 22 sheep. It looks like rain. Sure to have the sheep storm."

"Wednesday, June 15

Dull day. Put the sheep out in the woods. Spread 2 rows of manure. Russell gone to haul a load of lobsters to McLeod's factory. The wind has stopped around to the north west. There was a boat upset off MacLeod's factory. Man clung to bottom of boat and was saved. Planted 2 bushels of potatoes and tried to sow the turnips but it blowed too hard to sow them."

"Thursday, June 16

Fine day but very high wind. Blowing hard from the northwest and cold. I rolled the field of oats on the old place and sowed the turnips. Alexander is going to town with his ox. Russell is going to John Toombs. Fetched Hetty Houston here tonight. Her and Pensie are going to town tomorrow."

"Friday, June 17

Very cold day. High wind from the north. Our folk are all gone to the city to-day. Alexander with his ox and Russell with the wagon. Pensie has gone to get braws. I gave her fifty dollars. She will soon spend it."

"Saturday, June 18

Fine day. Went and put the sheep up at Montana. There is 21 sheep and 13 lambs. They had got into George Macneill's field and one sheep came home badly used up by dog. Put up a fence in clover field to make pasture for little pigs. Two men round looking after horses. They wanted to buy Jack but would not pay the figure. Went off telling me that I had lost a good offer. Went and fenced on the marsh. Came home to tea and the same men came back and paid the price and took the horse for $80.00."

"Sunday, June 19

Fine day. Preaching in Cavendish to-day. In Stanley this afternoon. The Foresters are going to march in procession clad in their badges. Mr. Robertson is going to preach to them. Our folk went to Stanley and came home disappointed. It is raining now. It is fine for the crop which seem to need it. Will Bulman is here and Hetty Houston. Mr. Robertson was down after cream."

"Monday, June 20

Fine day. Our folk commenced to send their milk to the factory this morning. Bob fetched very little whey. He says the can leaks. Sent it down to Mosey. Got it soldered. Cost 10 cts. Hetty Houston is here dress making."

"Tuesday, June 21

Rainy day. Not doing much. Cleaned up 14 bushels of wheat for mill + 6 bushels of oats. Campbell was here to-day begging flour to make bread and oats to feed his pig."

"Wednesday, June 22

Fine day but showering. I went over to New Glasgow to get the truck wagon repaired. Took them all day to fix it. They charged me $3.50 for the work they done which I think is very high. Came home by the New Bridge looking after peas. Could not find any. Mosey Doiron was boss in shop. Not a bad fellow."

"Thursday, June 23

Showery day. Sent a grist to the mill of 18 bushels of wheat and 8 bushels of oats for meal. George Macneill has commenced to put barbed wire along the road. He wants to sell the old mare. He wants 20 dollars for her. It is too much but she would be handy to hack about. Mrs. MacKenzie is on the rampage about pasture for her cows. She may get the wire if she likes. We harrowed the potatoes to-day. They are coming up well."

"Friday, June 24

Fine day. Boys top-dressing oats to-day with short manure. We covered a good piece of ground. Alexander has gone to Kensington after shingles and windows and lime. Took a box of feed to Aunt Ellie. Mr. Robertson and Mrs. Robertson were down after buttermilk. Joe Doucet was up after milk, eggs and butter. Alex brought 5 m of shingles at 1 dollar per m. and 2 windows and a cask of lime and 4 lbs. of paint."

"Saturday, June 25

Dull rainy day. Not doing much. I fixed the shingles on the barn and done up the chores. Lilly's children was here to dinner to-day. Mrs. Murray Robertson was here to dinner to-day. She fetched some rhubarb. She stayed till after tea. She weighs 149 lbs. Hetty Houston is going home tonight her work being done. Russell is going to take her home."

"Sunday, June 26

Rainy day. Preaching in Rustico to-day. Will went down. He is holy sometimes and very bad other times. Preaching at Cavendish tonight. Children gone to church."

"Monday, June 27

A fine day after the rain. We are doing up the chores around the place getting ready to whitewash."

"Tuesday, June 28

A fine day."

"Saturday, July 9

Fine day. Busy hoeing turnips. Murphy the blacksmith was here trying to sell a rake. Did not succeed. I went over and got the mare shod. Came home by Rustico and bought a bottle of harness blacking from Joseph Gallant. It cost 25 cts. Pensie and Bessy went down to Rustico to Ben's and Bulman's, Minnie's and Lelia's. She got a trace fixed at Nelson MacCoubrey's. Cost 15 cts."

"Sunday, July 10

A fine day. Preaching in Rustico to-day. Few at church from this way. Sermon in Cavendish this evening."

"Monday, July 11

Fine day. Hoeing turnips. Ground badly baked. Turnips do not seem to grow. Russell putting the scuffler through the potatoes. They have missed badly and appear stunted in their growth."

"Tuesday, July 12

A fine day. Busy hoeing potatoes and turnips. Had Mary Ann Penowe helping me. We finished the big field at 3 o'clock and came home and commenced on the field by the barn. There is a picnic down at the capes from Stanley Wedlock & Co. In all 5 wagons. Sold Davey Penowe 30 lbs. of floure at 2 1/4 cts per lb.

"Wednesday, July 13

A fine day. Busy hoeing turnips in field by barn till 4 o'clock. Then the people began to arrive for the wedding. Buntains, Letty, and Maria and Walter and Lorenzo and Minnie Toombs and child, Albert and Bessy and Letty, Oliver and Lelia, Willis Howard, wife and child, Miss Bulman and John McKie, Will Bowman, Mr. Robertson and son George and old Lapell selling ladders."

"Thursday, July 14

Fine day. Busy hoeing turnips. Had a visit from Ada Macneill. Started the mower in back field. Cut some of the heavy clover. Looks very like rain. Perhaps I did wrong by cutting at all till the weather settles. Alexander has gone over to New Glasgow with Pensie's things and Russell has taken her cow. She is very contrary and hard to drive. Albert was up after his chairs. I think that we have got all square again."

Friday, July 15

A very rainy day. The rain has fell in torrents most of the day and night. Very bad weather for the hay that is cut. Our field of clover will be saturated. It will likely be spoiled if it continues wet much longer. I was down at the shore this afternoon. Phil Doucet has just arrived with herring for bait. Lelia was up to-day. Boys down on road farm after hay poles."

"*Saturday, July 16*

Showery morning. Moved the sheep from Montana to the shore field. Hope they will do better now. Cleared up fine. Russell scuffling potatoes. Alexander not doing much. I am hoeing turnips. After that turning hay. It is very wet. Will try and rake it up this evening. Had 198 coils of hay. Very faire if saved well. Races up at J.T. Cosgroves to-day. Bad time there I hear. Too much beer and too little sense showed by people that ought to know better."

"*Sunday, July 17*

A very fine day. Wind northwest. Preaching in Cavendish to-day. Alex took McGill to church for the first time. Minnie was here this morning. She drove herself up. Fetched some lemons and sweeties. She is very kind. Pensie was in church to-day. She did not come home to see me. Perhaps the time may come she will wish she had."

"*Monday, July 18*

Fine day but very calm. Not very good for hay. We shook out the coils of hay two or three times and put in 5 loads of hay. I was down at Toph Penowe after the boy. Fetched him home with me. Mrs. George Macneill was here when I came home. She fetched over some strawberries. She is very kind. Campbell was away selling fish. I did not see him but his wife says he will come tomorrow."

"*Tuesday, July 19*

Cloudy day. Rained at 12 o'clock. Bad for the hay. Took in some hay this morning. Not fit for much. Joe and Mary Robertson was here after the ballance of cemetery fund being 68 cts. and 34 cts. that Russell owed for wire and posts that he bought at sale."

"*Wednesday, July 20*

Cloudy morning. Bad hay weather. I sowed 1/4 lb. of late turnip seed in a piece where the potatoes missed. Bad business when the potatoes is a failure. Commenced to work at hay after dinner. Had Campbell helping me. Took in about 10 loads in not very good condition. Campbell had his gun with him. He wants to sell it. He wants 10 dollars for it."

"*Thursday, July 21*

Rainy day. Can't touch the hay to-day. Hoeing turnips when we can. It is very showery. Lelia and her 2 children were here to-day. She got 12 lb. of wool. I charged her nothing for it. Russell went down to Toombs with 15 bushels of grain to get smashed. Pensie and Will Bulman was here tonight. They gave us

2 Mackerel. They bought them at the creek. Albert was up to change 5 dollars. I gave him $2.95 cts. The balance is 2.05."

"Friday, July 22

Cloudy morning with shower. I went to town after Pensie's furniture. Bought it at Newsome's. It cost 22 dollars. I started for home at 2 o'clock. Came home by the New Glasgow road. Got on well till I came to New Glasgow where Leander Macneill ran into my waggon and the mare started to run and threw me off the waggon but I held on to the reins and brought her to with a round turn. Got righted and came on to Bulman's and discharged cargo. Came home all right."

"Saturday, July 23

Fine day for hay. Have Campbell helping me. Leander Macneill came down to see me this morning. Glad to see him. Mrs. D. Penowe was here this day after flour for 1 dollar. Mrs. MacKenzie was here to-day and Bessy and Letty. Campbell was helping at the hay. Alex is off to old Hoops. He is not quite sound now. My back is very sore. No mail tonight."

"Sunday, July 24

Fine day. Preaching in Rustico to-day. Not many went down. Sharp shower at noon. My back is sore. I can hardly take my breath by times. Minnie and Ren was up to-day with all the children. They are all well. Glad to see them. Our people are off to Cavendish church tonight to hear the news and see the people."

"Monday, July 25

Fine day but very like rain. Russell put on Paris Green on Mrs. MacKenzie's potatoes. Mary Ann is hoeing turnips. We are taking in hay from the lower field. Took a load of hay to Mrs. Robertson's. Billy is putting the cart through his potatoes. My back is very sore."

"Tuesday, July 26

Fine day. Tea party at chapel to-day. Not very good weather for hay. Cutting the clover on the lower field."

Friday, November 4, 1898

Mr. George Macneill died this morning at 3 o'clock very suddenly. He complained of pain in side and he got up and tried to light the fire but could not. Mrs. Macneill was making him a drink when he fell over and expired. He never spoke after he fell."

Finis

L.M. Montgomery's Commentary on Charles Macneill's Diary From her journal entry dated March 1, 1925[1]

I have finished the old diary. It has taken me several Sunday afternoons and meanwhile I have been writing my journal entries separately and will copy them down later. To any other person in the world Charles Macneill's old diary would be tedious to read and unthinkably tedious to copy. But to me every moment I spent in copying it was a delight. I was back again in a world where happiness reigned and problems were non-existent—for me at least. I was so much at his home when a child and young girl that every word he wrote brought back vividly some sweet memory of those past days and childish frolics and delights. The most commonplace statement seemed like a finger touching the keys of an organ and evoking melodies of haunting sweetness—sights, sounds, of that old north shore farm that came back like the faint appealing voices of ghosts heard long ago many shadowy years agone. Pensie was alive to run with me under the moon and together we slipped back into that garden where the sword is set and mortals may not pass—the Eden of childhood.

I have copied the diary faithfully. Occasionally there is a mistake in the date or a mistake in spelling. But very few. Charles Macneill was a remarkably good writer and speller for a man who had had so little chance. Almost his only grammatical error is to use "was" with a plural subject. None of his family could do so well. They all seemed to take after their mother who was very illiterate, loveable and kind though she was.

Yes, every line has its charm for me. Charles writes that it is raining heavily. I am standing with Pensie at the front door of the little hall looking out over eastern Cavendish. The rain is coming down steadily over the wide green fields and the dark groves of spruce and the little golden dells between them. Far down "Angus MacKenzie's house" comes out against its emerald hill. Off to the left runs the sea, gray through the mist of rain—how did Tennyson put it?—"The sea's long level dim with rain"[2]—I recalled that line often when I looked at the sea from that old house on a rainy day. And the long red road growing darker and redder and richer under the wet. Sometimes he adds that it is thundering and I see the huge black clouds riding up over the tiny house

---

1 This is an excerpt from *The Complete Journals of L.M. Montgomery: The Ontario Years, 1922–1925* (Rock's Mills Press, 2018).

2 In fact these lines are from the first stanza of American poet John Greenleaf Whittier's (1807–92) poem, "The Last Walk in Autumn": "O'er the bare woods, whose outstretched hands / Plead with the leaden heavens in vain, / I see, beyond the valley lands, / The sea's long level dim with rain."

and the great willows behind it and Pensie and I run from the door and crouch in the parlor that has grown almost dark, and out to sea a shaft of lightning pierces the sky and the woods have grown dim in their skirts of shadow. Or he complains that it is very poor weather for haying. I see the great hayfields—riffling in the wind—lying in lustrous, fragrant swaths after mowing—covered with "coils" in the light of July sunsets—haunted and still on nights of white moon splendor. "Down home" the neat little cones into which the raked hay was hurriedly made up when rain threatened were always called "coils." Here in Ontario, that name is unknown. They are called "cocks." Many a time I have helped "coil" the hay, when a fine afternoon gave promise of a sudden shower and everybody was pressed into service to get the hay saved. It was not hard work—and the surroundings made it pleasant. I remember that Pensie and I coiled a whole field of hay one evening when the men were away and a thunderstorm was brewing. I don't think our coils were as perfectly shaped as Mr. Charles' would have been but they served. And now Pensie has been dead nearly twenty years.

"A fine clear day for harvest"—I see the sunlight falling over the fields "ripe unto harvest." I see the rows of "stooks"—"shocks" they call them here. I have "stooked" grain in my time, too—I see the bare stubble land after the big loads of grain have been hauled to the barn. I used to build a load now and then myself. There was an art in it. If the load were not properly built it was apt to collapse before it got to the barn and cover the builder with ignominy. Of course I never had much of this sort of work to do but almost every summer there came an afternoon when rain threatened and men were scarce and "we youngsters" were pressed into emergency service. I never "built" a load of hay. But a load of sheaves was not such a hard thing to build if you were careful to "bind" it properly with the end sheaves as you went along and didn't get it too wide or too narrow or too top-heavy or too loose.

Or perhaps the "rain" comes on Sunday, while the people are at "preaching." I am back in the old Presbyterian church in Cavendish. I am sitting in the pew between Grandmother and Grandfather. Right before me in the front pew sit Amanda and Tillie and old Aunt Caroline[3] of the quilted black satin bonnet. Far back under the gallery in one of the post seats Mr. Charles is sitting, his shock of bushy gray hair standing stiffly up above his gray bearded face. Everybody else is there. Folks dead and buried for a quarter of a century hurry out of their graves and come to fill their pews just because I read in an old diary that it "rained at preaching." Not one is missing from "old McKinstrie," in the front centre pew to "old Willie Makum," twisting his face into weird grimaces away up in his gallery pew. Mr. Archibald is preaching and

---

3   Aunt Caroline was Charles Macneill's unmarried sister. See note 9, page 18 (July 28, 1923).

the choir are all in their places in the front pew of the gallery. Rain is beating against the high, narrow white-glass windows. The wind is wailing mournfully around the church. I look out of the window so blessedly near our pew. The long grasses in the graveyard are tossing in the wind or lying down wetly under the downpour. The pond is gray down in the valley, the sand hills can be hardly seen for rain—the sea beyond moans on its rocky shore. The horses tied to the graveyard fence don't like the rain. But the wet landscape has a charm all its own. After all, I rather like it when it "rains at preaching."

Or perhaps it is just "blowing hard." Perhaps the wind is north. Then it comes swooping up from the shore right through Charles' yard and whistles about his doorstep. Away out the gulf is dotted all over with white caps. Near in to shore just beyond the green fields is a line of breakers under a mist of foam. But if it is northwest or west the little house is so well sheltered by the "bush" to the back of it that we don't feel the wind. It only thrashes the tops of the trees and howls in the dog-woods. But it may be south or southwest and then it is a lonesome thing, purring softly down over the slopes behind the house and laughing in the garden and blowing leaves crazily across the yard. Or it is east—sad, mournful, blowing up from "a gray and haunted shore." And night comes down with the blackness of the wild autumn storms and Pensie and I scurry into the house and shut the door, laughing, in its face. Pensie with her pretty auburn curls and her roguish face. Who

Old Cavendish Church

said she was dead? I saw her but a moment ago. As Kipling says, "The Lords of life and death shut the doors behind us"[4]—but sometimes they swing open for a minute and the ghostly hands of winds that blew forty years ago play with our hair again.

Or it is "a fine bright day." Who should know better than I what "a fine bright" August day on that old north shore was? Air crystal and golden. Vast sky gardens where white cloud flowers bloomed. Great golden fields with the magic of dark spruce woods behind them. Musky, spicy garden flowers. Triangles of sea shimmering into violet; faint blue loveliness over New London harbor: "authentic music of eternity" echoing up from the rocky shore. Yes, it is indeed a fine bright day. There are days like that there yet. We never have

---

4   From Rudyard Kipling's short story, "The Finest Story in the World," from his 1890 collection, *Indian Tales*.

just that kind of day inland. Only the sea can give them.

Or a November entry says "snowed in the night." The first snow of the winter that is to be. At sunset the world was gray and ugly. At sunrise it is a fair white thing and the sea looks blackly gray and dour by contrast. The ploughed fields are all dimpled; the spruces and firs are as white palms; the apple trees still holding their withered leaves look blossom-gay again. Only they are all white. There are no pink hearts. But as the day wears on it gets "sloppy." The snow melts and the beauty vanishes.

In December there is "a fine day with squalls of snow by times." Yes, I remember that kind of day, too. Ground frozen hard. Biting wind in spite of the sunshine. Up comes a big black cloud. A wave of gray shadow goes over the world. Then the stinging drive of sudden snow. The air is a wild white blur with it. The fields whiten, the hills grow pale. Presto, the cloud is gone. The sun is out. But winter is a little nearer. Then comes an entry, "Froze hard last night. Roads very rough." Bumpy driving over them now. Pensie and I give up our out door prowls and keep to the house when I visit there. But when I go home in the wintry twilight there is something nice in tramping along over the hard firm road. No mud now. Household lights gleaming warmly out along the road. Melody of storm in the wind that is swooping down over the sleeping fields; a big round silvery moon floating up over a frosty hill; the gnomish beauty of dark lombardies against the moonrise; bars of moonlight and shadow on the road under the trees and Pensie beside me—always laughing. Do the dead laugh?

In January are many "cold" entries. "As the days begin to lengthen the cold begins to strengthen" says Grandfather Macneill, quoting a saw of his father, who doubtless had it from *his* father. I wonder who first invented the little rhyme. I recall the odd sudden childish rebellion that always flamed up in my soul when I heard it. I hated it; and yet it *was* true—for a time. The cold *did* strengthen in January and February; and the storms came whirling over the fields and heaping drifts along the fences and fiercely bombarding the little house crouching against its friendly sheltering "bush." But they died at its door. Inside it was always the cosiest, warmest, snuggest, little place. Sitting room and parlor heated by roaring stoves. What matter if it were "very cold" outside?

But even in January comes sometimes "a mild day" and "a white frost." What a pretty name is "white frost." And the thing itself—lovely as some whim of wildwood god. Every tree a miracle—every dead weed and blade of grass a wonder. The great willows arching over the little house things of silver and pearl; the shrubs in the garden and the underbrush in the grove fairy jungles.

Then in March come the "blustery days"—"the windy days," "the mild days." April brings rain and bad roads; and in May there is a "foggy day." How

I used to love foggy days. For me there was always a beauty and a mystery in the fog of that north shore. An evening fog filled me with a strange deep joy—that mournful ghostly thing hanging low over the fields and drifting in phantom-like waves through the spruces. But Pensie is laughing. I hear her telling a joke. An old man drives into the yard and greets her father. "Fogging, sir." We have never heard "fogging" before. We think it is exquisitely funny. Thereafter we never meet each other on a misty day without saying "Fogging, sir." And why not? As well as raining and blowing? Yes, I loved days when it "fogged."

"Mr. Charles" has "built a stack." Again a host of memory pictures. One never sees stacks in Ontario. The barns here are so large they can hold all the hay and grain. The smaller P.E.I. barns could not and when there was a generous crop some of it must be "stacked." Sometimes the stack was built in the field itself and hauled home by sleighloads in winter. Often the grain or hay was hauled to the farm-yard and a group of stacks built in some sheltered place. These groups had a certain fascination for me, especially in a winter twilight when they were coated with snow and seemed to shoulder each other in the shadows. Or at night with a pale moon-glow behind them. I never took part in building a stack—that was only for experts; but I recall one afternoon when Pensie and I climbed up on a half-finished stack and lay there in the fragrant clover talking girlish secrets with the blue sky over us and the cool delicious gulf breeze blowing around us, bringing with it all kinds of elusive whiffs from all the little dells and slopes of the old farm.

One day Mr. Charles has one brief entry and one alone. "Stumping."[5] After a man had been stumping all day he did not feel much like diary writing. He was thankful to go to bed, feeling that some stumps attempted, some stumps done had earned a night's repose. Mr. Charles "stumped" a little every summer and cleared a bit more fertile land. But there were always enough stumps left in the "back fields" to provide delightful berrying grounds for us. Nowhere were there more delightful spots than among the stumps, nowhere places were berries bigger and redder or more abundant than among the long grasses and the clumps of fern.

One day he "puts up a stack of hay in Montana." Montana! That was what they called the acres of stumps over grown with a second growth of young maple at the "backest back." Why, I don't know. But I knew every winding path and maple clump and young fir group and fern-filled hollow in that beautiful place and I am in it again just because of its mention in Mr. Charles' diary.

"Albert went to Kensington after binder twine."[6] An entry that connotes a certain change that had come into farm life, doing away with much hard work

---

5   Stumping consisted of removing tree stumps to enlarge fields for tillage.

6   Used to fasten hay or straw into bales that could be stacked in a barn.

and also with much romance and beauty. The advent of the "self-binder."

I do not of course remember the day of the reaping hook. But when I was a very small girl Grandfather had an old-fashioned mowing machine. On it were two seats—one for the driver, the other for a second man, holding a wooden rake in his hand, whose duty it was to rake off the sheaves, using his own judgment as to when enough grain had fallen on the board from the knives to make a sheaf. I have heard Grandfather say what a wonderful invention they thought this when it came first. But it was now out-of-date and very soon a new mower was bought, with revolving rakes that went round and round until, when the driver touched a spring, one rake fell lower than the others and swept off the sheaves. This was thought another wonderful contrivance. But the sheaves had to be bound and for this extra "hands" were hired—mostly black-eyed French girls who bound quickly and chattered ceaselessly in their patois. I found a great fascination in watching them and I longed to know how to make the "bands" but nobody ever would teach me. A girl would catch up a cluster of grain, twist it with another cluster in a special knot, gather up the sheaf and knot the "band" around it in a twinkling. They did it so quickly my eye could never follow the motion and to this day the secret of the knot is unknown to me. I wonder if anyone living knows it or has it become one of the "lost arts."

Then came the self-binder—and the laughing, chattering "binders" vanished forever from the harvest fields by the gulf. The day of "binder twine" had come—and one more bit of poetry vanished from the world. And was anybody a whit the happier for the self binder? As for all the flood of machinery inventive "genius" has let loose upon the world?

"Alexander and Pensie and Maud went to the English church to-day." This is the only time I am mentioned in the diary. A reference elsewhere to "Maud playing the organ" is meant for Maud Macneill. But it is the mention of the English Church that touches the secret spring. The English church—as it was always called then. It is Anglican now;[7]—was at South Rustico about half way between Cavendish and Charlottetown. It always had a charm for me—an old gray church set back on a side road amid big trees, with a graveyard all around it. I did not get there very often but sometimes Alec and Pensie and I drove down to it on a summer Sunday evening. Great Grandfather Woolner[8] was buried there and his wife. I remember that on this particular evening Mr. Charles commemorates it began to rain and we had a wet drive. But I do not recall that it damped our spirits in the least. It seems to me that, when Alec and Pensie and I were on any jaunt, we laughed incessantly. Well, in those days most people with whom I foregathered did laugh, if they were any

---

7   St. Mark's Anglican Church in South Rustico, established in 1848; it was torn down in 2016.

8   Robert Chester Woolner (1787–1860) was born in Dunwich, England, and emigrated to PEI.

connection of the race of Joseph. I take some credit to myself for it. I had a knack of saying funny things about everything we saw or heard that kept my companions in agonies of mirth—and no jokes ever got by me. I think I have some of the power left yet; but I seldom get any chance nowadays to exercise it. Only when I go back to Cavendish and sit with Alec and May around their supper table do I discover that I can still make people laugh.

Mr. Charles has several references to "the road farm." This is another phrase which, quite pithless to most readers, is a master key for me, opening another door into the past. This road farm was "a parcel of land" lying along the side road that led from the "Rustico Road" down to the eastern shore where were the remote farms of the Bernards, the Flemings and "Sandy Laird on the Capes." This road led through woods and clearings almost its whole length and was a wild and beautiful spot. I remember the first time I saw it; and that is linked with another memory. Pensie and I are sitting together in school one rough winter day. Amanda is not there. Very few pupils are there. So Pensie and I are sitting together in the old "back seat" where the desks were so high that almost anything could be done behind them. But Pensie and I are not doing anything very dreadful. We are writing "letters" to each other on our slates. I don't know why we are not doing arithmetic or studying our lesson. Let the teacher answer. We finish the letters and exchange slates. Pensie writes me about a certain plan of ours—to wit, that when spring comes we will walk down to Oliver Bernard's (Oliver was married to her sister Lily). Pensie describes the road we will take—"such a pretty road"—ferns all along it, trees meeting overhead etc. I am intrigued. From that moment I look forward hungrily to our walk. In due time it comes. One rare spring day we walk down. For once realization is every whit as sweet as anticipation. The road *is* lovely. Ferns in clumps and ferns in curly masses and lonely upstanding brackens; masses of purple rhododendrons—"sheep laurel." Mayflower stars along the way; blue and white violets; strawberry blossoms; clumps of young maple; slender firs; bird calls; wild fragrances; squirrels chattering secrets of Polichinelle;[9] stipplings of sunlight along the moist red road; wine of spring in the crystal air; hill glamor and upland magic; an immortal spirit of beauty brooding over everything; Pensie and I faring on together, feeling adventurous and expectant. No cares—no worries—not a bit afraid of tomorrow.

But Pensie is dead; and I am inclined to think that the road has been "cleared" and is nothing now but a road instead of being, as it was then, a highway in the land of faery.

Mr. Charles has "stooked" a wheat field up complete. I see it, lying in autumnal sunlight, dotted over with the golden stooks—"shocks" they call them

---

9   "Polichinelle" is the name of a character from Italian *Commedia dell'arte*.

in Ontario. I have done a little "stooking" in my time too. It was not hard work. A field of stooks in moonlight was always a place of faery and gramarye.[10]

"Taking in wheat from the old place." Chas. Macneill was a thrifty soul and he had accumulated goodly acres. Besides the "home place" he had the "road farm" and "the old place" which is now Alec's farm. It was called the old place because his uncle, "Old Chas." Macneill, had once owned it. Before this time he had also owned the farm which is now Albert's and after this he rented the "old Ewan McKenzie place." He was a tireless steady worker and a good manager. I know of no man who enjoyed farming more truly than old Mr. Charles. He rose while it was yet night and looked well to the ways of his farmyard and stables. One record has it that he got up at 2 o'clock to take in a field of wheat because it looked like rain.

One entry "got the mill for to thrash" revives another host of memories. In those days in Cavendish everybody had his crop thrashed by a little two-horse-power "threshing machine." I think most of them have gasoline engines now. Here in Ontario all the threshing is done in a day or two by a gang and a steam engine.

In those old days we small fry were vastly excited when the threshing days came. Generally we had to stay home from school to "tramp straw." Albert Macneill had a mill and he went around to thresh for his neighbors. His job was to "feed the drum." Sometimes he cut the bands also and then someone had to pass him the sheaves one by one from the piles in which they were pitched down from the loft. I often did this and loved to do it. To watch the great ravenous teeth of the "drum" catch and rend and tear the sheaf as Albert "fed" it had a terrible fascination for me. So many sheaves made a "rally"—I don't know how many. After each "rally" horses and men had a rest of ten minutes or so. But perhaps I was not passing sheaves but was "tramping" straw in loft or outside stack or shed. This was necessary in order to pack the straw and make room for it all. It was gorgeous fun. I loved it all—the whir and roar and dust—and the clouds of grain pouring out of the drum, while the straw was coughed furiously out beyond to the waiting man with the fork who tossed it to us. The only drawback to it all was the mice. There were always legions of them, especially when the lower layers of sheaves were reached.

Pensie and I, I remember, loved to get on the wooden tread of the mill, when it would be standing idle before their barn, and make it go. We always had to get one of the boys to start it first but once started we could keep it going as long as our legs lasted. If we had been compelled to do this we would have howled in protest; but when it was play—why, it *was* play. And if I had "growing pains" that night when I went to bed—why, everybody had to have

---

10   "Stooking" referred to creating a field stack of small rectangular bales of hay or straw. "Gramarye" is a Middle English word for occult learning or magic.

growing pains. One must grow.

There are some rather pathetic little entries about his eye. Eventually he lost the sight of it completely but then it ceased to be painful and the other remained good to his end. In one entry he writes "It is hard to be afflicted thus." No doubt it was. And yet Charles Macneill had a life almost free from trouble and illness. I never knew of his being ill until the time of his death came and this trouble in his eye was the only physical affliction he ever had. His family all turned out decently and there was no break in it until Pensie's death which came a year or two before his own. His life was a very narrow one but in its groove, it was as happy, peaceful and prosperous a one as I ever knew.

The entry "hauling old longers for firewood" reminds me of the fact that I have never heard the old rails of fences called "longers" (pronounced longgers) any place outside of P.E. Island. I have never come across it in any literature, not even in dialect. Yet they were always called so on the Island. The derivation must have been English or Scotch. Yet I suppose neither in England nor Scotland were there ever any fences of that kind, so one is forced back on an American or Canadian derivation. The "poles" which Mr. Chas. often cuts in his diary, were much slighter, shorter affairs, used for the ends of the "longers" to rest on. In my childhood these pole and longer fences were all there were, save back in the clearings where some "stump fences" were found. Occasionally some fiendish creature built what was called a "picket fence" or a "pitchpole" fence. This was built entirely of "poles" driven into the ground at an angle, their sharp points sticking up all along the top. You couldn't climb it or wriggle through it. Therefore we berry pickers hated it and anathematized the builders thereof. Then "board fences" came in but were too expensive to oust the longer fence entirely. And then the hideous, horrible barbed wire, which being cheap was soon met with everywhere. I *have* managed to climb a barbed wire fence but it was not a joke. And it was impossible to slide between the wires as we did in the plain wire fences of a later day.

The old "snake" longer fence was a beautiful thing in its way, though wasteful of land. In the angles formed by the longers such beautiful things grew. Long, purple-plumed wild grasses, ferns, bracken, strawberry vines, daisies, fireweed, farewell-summers, yarrow, "life-o'-man" and great armies of golden rod. Even in winter the gray-headed golden-rods stuck up through the snowdrifts that always filled up those corners.

There were stone "dykes" there, too, and they were beautiful things when they grew old. The custom was brought out from Scotland. The dykes were built of layers of the red stones picked off the fields alternated with layers of sods. Soon the grass growing from the sods covered the stones, and if it didn't mosses and lichen did. Then dear things took root in the crevices among the stones and wove beauty about the old dykes—flowers and ferns and mosses and berries. An old dyke was an amazing place for strawberries, with stems so long that you could pick a "bouquet" of them. And there were always bird's nests in the holes among the stones. A low fence was built along the top of the dyke or a hedge of spruce trees planted. If they were not planted they sprang up and grew anyway. Oh, those old dykes were the most lovable things. Our old farm was full of them. A dyke ran down right from "Jimmy Laird's line" along the main road to our gate. Another one, covered with wild rose bushes, bounded the field by the church. Our front orchard was surrounded by one, so old and overgrown that it looked like a bank of earth and huge trees grew out of it. The whole road down to the shore had a dyke along one side of it—a dyke where I have picked quarts of strawberries on summer evenings. Amanda's old lane was dyked on both sides—a dyke famous for the "sours" which we loved to eat. To speak of a barbed wire fence in the same breath with one of those exquisite, poesy-haunted old dykes were to commit sacrilege.

Verily, the fact that Mr. Chas. "hauled longers" one day over thirty years ago and wrote it down has led me far afield—into old fields, lying in the light of faraway summers, hemmed in by dykes or silver-gray longers and gaining from them a certain racy individuality and charm no wire-girdled meadow could ever know or possess.

The cheapness of things in those days is a constant marvel to me now. One day Mr. Charles went to the shore and bought three mackerel. For these three mackerel he paid the huge sum of 8 cents. They would make a good dinner for his whole family. Today those same three mackerel would be at least a dollar and probably more.

It is odd how our tastes change as we grow older—not only mentally but physically. When I was a child I could not eat mackerel—fresh mackerel at least. I always loved the delicious broiled salt mackerel. But the fried fresh mackerel which almost everyone thought so delicious I could not eat at all. Now I love it. I always liked fresh codfish. No one knows what fresh codfish is really like except one who has eaten it with only an hour between sea and pot. Those great snow-white slices of codfish served up with Grandmother's "drawn butter" sauce.[11] Food for gods! Nothing to equal them save the trout Uncle Leander caught in the pond. There is a flavor about salt water fish that no fresh water fish ever possesses. Codfish dried and broiled was a great breakfast and supper dish. They were spread on constructions called "flakes" and turned carefully until dry. It was an art not to let them get "sunburned" which ruined them.

People who have been dead and forgotten for a generation live in this diary of old Mr. Charles. He mentions "James McKinstrie"—and instantly I see him. A little white haired old Scotchman sitting every Sunday in the "top middle

---

11   A sauce made with butter, onions, and cornstarch.

pew" of old Cavendish church. He was born in Scotland and never lost the Lowland "brogue." He was an eccentric individual and there was always some tale of "old McKinstrie's" utterances floating round. He had considerable native intelligence but was entirely uneducated. In short, he might have stepped out of one of Scott's novels. The type is never seen today.

Scattered all through the diary are the French names—Mr. Charles does not always spell them right—which were so well-known to my childhood. Gautiers (we called it "Goachy"), Peters, Blacquiere (Blackair), Pineau (Mr. Charles has it Penowe), Gallant (Gallong), Doucet, Doiron, Poirier (Perry), Buote (Be-ot) and so on. And the first names. Silvien, Francois, Maxim, Peter (Peter Peters was a red-headed Frenchman who used to work for Grandfather), Leon, Napoleon (generally "Pullyong"), Zebedee (always "Zeb") and a host of Scripture names—Moses, Jeremiah, David, Matthew, Paul etc. etc. etc. Grandfather always had a "hired boy" in the summer. From May to November the wages paid those boys in those days were $36. Thirty six dollars for a whole summer. Nowadays they want that a month! Nor did they think themselves abused. I always liked our French folk. They were generally a good-natured, happy-go-lucky obliging lot. The only thing I disliked was a certain smutty streak which was carefully concealed from our older people but was now and then allowed to peep out before us children.

"Cleaning out the greenhouse" does not refer to a conservatory. The "greenhouse" at Mr. Chas. was a deep pit dug in the ground with a wooden roof built over it, in which vegetables were stored, generally those intended for the stock. People did not have cement stables in those days and the cellars of the houses could not hold all the crop. So they built what were called "greenhouses," though the name was certainly a misnomer.

"Nobody travelling. Times very dull." Mr. Charles did not like it when nobody was travelling. No one liked better than he to see folks drop in. He counted that day lost whose low-descending sun had not shone on some begging or borrowing Frenchman, some strolling peddler, or some neighbor, even if he might write a sarcastic sentence about them in his diary that evening. He loved to talk to everyone, getting all the local news. You always heard all the current gossip at "Charles's." They were not malicious. But they never read books or papers and their only amusement was their interest in the doings of their small world. They had a spy-glass in the house and it was invariably trained on everybody who walked or drove down the road. I never went down that road in daytime without feeling that spy glass focused on the small of my back. It was a local joke.

Mr. Charles buys "a load of seaweed" from a certain Toph Pinneau—"Toph" being short for Theophilus. In the autumns of those days everyone had to haul or buy seaweed to "bank the house for the winter." It was a November job. The whole house was encircled by a girdle of sea-weed, held in by stakes and "longers." The more seaweed you could command the higher and wider your "banking." I remember Uncle John Montgomery up at Princetown used to have the house banked to the windowsills. It certainly made it warm for the winter. I don't really know if they bank with seaweed on the Island now or not. A great many people "bank" now with sods or clay—as the unfortunates of forty years ago who lived too far inland to get seaweed had to do them.

"Took the sleighs out of stable, box and wood."

There were three classes of "sleighs" in common use in those days. The "jaunting sleigh"—the name "cutter" was never heard then—which was used for light travelling and always by canoodling couples. The "box sleigh"—or "pung" as it later came to be called. A rather comfortable affair which might have a seat in front or might have no seat at all. In that case it was filled with straw, covered with a buffalo or rug. You all hopped in and squatted down— half a dozen of you. I've had more fun in those old "box sleighs" than in any other form of conveyance—especially on moonlit winter nights on the road to some party or "meeting," when everyone in the sleigh was under twenty. The "wood" sleigh—so called because used for hauling wood, was merely a low frame on runners, sometimes with a loose board or two laid on it, with stakes at the four corners connected by chains. When the sleigh was empty the driver rode standing and it must have been quite an art to balance yourself. There were also "mud" sleighs—wood sleighs with huge wooden boxes very deep, on them, used for hauling home the loads of mud which were dug from the oyster beds in winter. Later on "toboggans" became very fashionable—not quite so "classy" as jaunting sleighs but much "classier" than the box and much affected by young lads who could not aspire to a jaunting sleigh but wanted some vehicle to drive their lady friends about in. At Charles', Alec drove the jaunting sleigh, Russell drove the toboggan and the old folks were generally contented with the homely reliable "box."

In winter days Mr. Charles spent much time in the woods cutting firewood. They never burned anything but wood. The woodpile was always to the left of the kitchen door. In the tiny kitchen was an old Waterloo Stove. When Pensie and I came in from coasting or sliding with cold toes we sat before it and warmed them on the hot hearth. Sometimes we roasted corn cobs over the glowing coals. That little house was plain and homely but it was snug and warm. The "sitting room" and parlor were heated by stoves with doors that slid open revealing the glowing flames within. They were quite as beautiful and companionable as fire places. Off the parlor was the "spare bedroom." The tiniest place. Behind the door the bed filled up the whole side of the room. The bureau was in the corner opposite the door. There was one window looking out under the big willows into the garden. Many a night Pensie and I spent in that cosy bed, talking over our girlish secrets. And I have one sweet memory that seems to stand out more clearly than all the others. To this day it gives me the most delightful feeling whenever I recall it.

It was a cold winter night and good "Mrs. Charles" had come in with her candle to see if we were warm enough before she went to bed. Pensie was asleep but I was not, though I pretended to be, curled down among my pillows with closed eyes. Mrs. Charles bent over us. "Dear little children," she said gently and tenderly.

That was all. Mrs. Charles has been for many years in her grave. She was a very illiterate, simple-minded woman from whose lips no pearls of wisdom or jewels of inspiration ever dropped. But I have forgotten most of the wisdom and culture I have listened to; and I shall never forget those three simple words of love. I came from a household where affection was never expressed in words. Stern Grandfather, reserved Grandmother would never have said to me "dear little child" even had they felt it. And I loved such expression—I craved it. I have never forgotten it.

Poor Mrs. Charles never got over Pensie's death. Pensie was the only one of her family who had died. Whenever she saw me afterwards she would talk to me by the hour about her—"because you and her were such friends." She and Pensie are together now—if indeed "there be a land of souls beyond that sable shore."[12] And, if there be, I hope Mrs. Charles will come to me there, with Pensie, and look lovingly at us and say "dear little children" in just the same tone she said it that winter night of long ago. Oh, people should say things like that to children—little speeches of love and tenderness. They are more precious than rubies to small souls.

Mr. Charles never expressed his affection—if he felt any. One would never guess from his entry, "Ren Toombs' child died to-day,"[13] that the said child of the said Ren Toombs was his own grandson. This curious indifference runs through all his entries regarding his family. Perhaps it was only because he "being Scotch" could not put his feelings into words, especially cold-blooded written words. But somehow I do not think he was very deeply attached to anyone even his own children, despite his hospitality and kindness. Whenever "ma" went away for a day or two he wrote nasty little slurs in his diary about her. He seemed to resent her absences, instead of being glad that the poor soul had those few brief and seldom releases from the monotony of her busy days. But perhaps I am unjust to him in this. It maybe that these little spiteful entries of his concerning poor "ma's" little holidays were merely the result of his loneliness when she was away. Perhaps he missed her so much that he resented the pain and transferred his resentment unconsciously to her. He would never admit, not even to himself, that he missed her unbearably but his

---

12   From Byron's *Childe Harold's Pilgrimmage*, Canto II, stanza 8.
13   Lorenzo Toombs was a Cavendish neighbour.

discomfort had to have this queer distorted outlet. Believing this I can laugh over the entry, "Ma not home yet. Nearly as crazy as the Toombs." And a day or so later, "She'd better stay with the Toombs altogether."

Minnie's baby—her first-born—had died and her mother was staying a few days with her to help and comfort her. I fear we can't exonerate Mr. Charles completely from the charge of selfishness!

And he was always very satirical about his boy's little outings. He had an odd habit of writing that they had "gone on a mission" to the Scotch or "the American Jews" when they took some of their lady friends driving. Those boys were all steady hard-working fellows whose liveliest dissipation was a concert or pie-social. But Mr. Charles always waxed sarcastic when they had driven off and he sat him down to write in his little diary. I suppose they did run around a good deal. After working hard all day they wanted a little amusement and as they cared nothing for books had to seek it elsewhere. But it is killing to read all the "old man's" biting sentences about their gadding!

His three sons and his three daughters all married and "settled down" near to him. None of them ever seemed to have any desire to go afield—except Robbie. "Rob" was the second oldest boy; and he went clear across the continent to the Pacific coast and settled on a farm in the state of Washington. He was never home but twice afterwards. I do not think he has done any better or is any better off than if he had stuck to the old Island. Rob was more like his father than any of the others—which was probably why he could not get on as well with him. At all events, he left home because, he said, he could not "get a square deal."

"Took a load of wood to Alexander M. Macneill's."[14] Mr. Chas. brought us up a load of wood every winter in return for sundry bags and baskets of apples in autumn days. But the peculiarity of this entry is that Grandfather was Charles' uncle and one wonders why he did not write "Uncle Alexander" as he always called him. Did he feel that it would be tempting who knew what principalities and powers if he wrote too familiarly of his relatives?

Mr. Charles had his share of the Macneill jealousy. He did not like to think that any of his circle was doing better or even quite as well as he himself was. Not even when it was his own son-in-law. This is why, when he writes that Oliver Bernard was "hauling mud" he adds dryly, "Expects to be rich soon."

Of course Oliver Bernard *was* a terrible "blow" and none of his wife's family ever liked him. They were not at all well pleased when Lily married him, though he was a steady fellow with a comfortable home. They just didn't "like" him, that was all and they never did like him. But that didn't justify a "poison mean" trick that Albert played on him once when he was courting Lily. It was

---

14   That is, Alexander Marquis Macneill (1820–98), LMM's grandfather.

Henry MacLure told me this. One night he went home with Albert from some revelry and stayed all night with him. It was late—about twelve o'clock. Everyone was in bed except Lily who was "sitting up" with Oliver B. in the parlor. Albert inferred this because a brand-new overcoat of Oliver's was hanging on the sitting room wall. Albert went into the pantry, brought out a big bowl full of beets in vinegar and poured the whole mess into one of the pockets of the overcoat!

What was the sequel, if any, I never heard. Probably Oliver swallowed the insult for love's sweet sake. Anyhow, nothing redder than the beet vinegar flowed because of it. Yet dynasties have fallen for less.

Mr. Charles liked a sly slap at a minister now and then. One entry reads, "Mr. George was here to-day. He talked politics most of the time he was here. Did not say anything about religion or the one thing needful."

Mr. George was the minister who "supplied" Cavendish the winter after Mr. Archibald went away. As for Mr. Charles, he was by no means the spiritual person one might suspect from that entry. Religion to him meant going to church on Sundays and paying so much to the minister's salary. If Mr. George had talked religion to him he would have been the most uncomfortable man alive. I fancy Mr. George's complexion in politics did not commend itself to Mr. Charles!

Some of Mr. Charles' entries regarding "pigs" and "sows" are amusingly naive. Mr. Charles generally kept what was alluded to in a hushed voice—among women folk at least—as a "boar." This involved various mysterious visits from neighbors and Mr. Charles has them all marked down in his diary. Probably his reason was to keep track of such services until the fees were paid but they make rather comical entries, cheek by jowl with his hints about religion and his Sunday texts!

Mr. Chas. had his own private nicknames for people. Who "Long 5 axe handles" was I have no earthly idea but I strongly suspect that "Johnny Big-eyes" was Uncle John F.

"Too much bushel for a small canoe" was an old Indian proverb. I had heard it in my childhood but had forgotten it until it popped up again in the diary. Very expressive I think. Today we say "he bit off more than he can chew" but I like the Indian version better. I think the entry he makes regarding Russell, "too big for his pants," was of native manufacture. Certainly Mr. Chas. does not in this diary appear to be an overfond or over-proud parent.

"Hauling dulse" brings a whiff of salt air from the gulf. Two kinds of things were called "dulse." One was the long semi-transparent ribbons of real dulse which were regarded as quite a dainty. We picked them up on the shore, wet and glistening and ate them. Many people really liked them. I only pretended to.

The other dulse was the heaps of sea-plants that piled up on the shore after certain storms—mostly I think from the east. It was composed of real dulse, kelp—how pretty some forms of kelp were, especially the long strips that looked like shirred brown silk ribbon—Irish moss and all kinds of sea-weeds, and was an excellent fertilizer. When the word came that dulse was "in" every farmer whose land ran out to the gulf hurried to the shore with carts and hauled industriously.

Very delicious blanc-mange could be made from the Irish Moss—which was a pretty feathery thing when it was fresh and wet ranging through all colors—green, brown, pink, cream. Another variety of sea-weed bore bunches of little bladder-like fruit which burst with a report when you squeezed them. And there was a kelp like a long brown sea-snake.

An April entry, "Ice on shore," brings me back to the gulf. Springs in Cavendish were late or early according to the time the ice "went out." All winter the gulf was white with ice. But when spring winds began to blow a blue rift appeared here and there; and some fine day with a strong wind from the south away it all went. As long as the ice was "on shore" the weather would be cold and the green of field and woods reluctant to appear. Sometimes after the ice had been gone for two or three weeks we would see an odd, white streak far out on the northern horizon and say with a shiver, "The ice is coming back." Sometimes it would come clean into the shore again. And when it did it generally brought seals with it and the farmers would chase and capture them. The skin of that kind of seal was of no value but enormous quantities of oil could be obtained from the carcass and a farmer was lucky if he captured a seal or two. I recall a particularly huge one Grandfather caught. Its white and gray hide was nailed to the side of the barn to dry and I always see it when I hear the expression, "There'll be hides on the barn-door."

When Mr. Charles wished to express neighborly kindness in any way he "said it with wood." When anyone was sick Mr. Charles took them a load of wood. When anyone died Mr. Chas. sent them a load of wood. Well, a load of Mr. Charles' good hardwood was not a bad thing to have on hand—especially when much cooking had to be done for a funeral! It would really be of much more use than an anchor of roses or a pillow of white hyacinths.

He frequently uses the word "chores." I think they were the only family in Cavendish that used that word. Everywhere else the expression was "turns." It was only after some of the girls who had gone to Boston to work came back with new words that "chores" came into general circulation. The older folks did not adopt it, except Mr. Charles. No "Yankeeisms" for them. Grandfather and his contemporaries "did the turns" to the day of their deaths.

One Saturday Mr. Chas. cuts wood "for Sunday." Of course this was always done. One might cook a big dinner on Sunday and have half one's friendly circle in to help eat it but it was an unpardonable sin to cut wood on "The Lord's day." I remember a clan story that was always being told of Grandfather Montgomery. He was the soul of hospitality and always had a houseful of guests on Sunday. One Sunday an appalling discovery was made. By some oversight the wood had not been chopped on Saturday. There was no wood to cook the dinner. Grandfather rose to the occasion. "Boys," he said quietly to my father and Uncle Jim, "go out and *break a little with the back of the axe*"!!!

I don't know who the "two she-weasels" were who were around asking for money to buy the minister a fur coat! Either Mr. Charles did not like parting with his hard earned dollars to buy fur coats for ministers or—as was more likely—he did not like the ladies themselves. But he would be very agreeable to their faces, for all that and would send them on their way rejoicing. Then he would relieve his feelings and escape a complex by calling them she-weasels in his diary! Perhaps he was in a bad humor that day. Next day or so two other ladies arrived collecting money for a present to the school teacher. Mr. Charles let them off with "beggars." Somehow, "beggars" sounds very savorless after "she weasels."

One naive little entry amused me. "Letty was here to-day. She is very smart. Gave her ten cents for Christmas." Letty was his little granddaughter, then about two or three years old. "Ten cents" does not seem a very lavish Christmas gift. But I recall that when I was a small girl ten cents seemed a quite munificent sum indeed. In fact, as far as actual money goes it was worth as much as thirty or forty today, and to have a whole "ten cent piece"—one never heard of dimes in those days—to spend and no questions asked was wealth.

Mr. Charles gives poor Aunt Ann Maria a fearful slam in one of his entries. She has "got a new fur coat and if she could get a new set of brains might do very well for a while."

Well, brains were certainly not poor Aunt Ann Maria's long suit. She had absolutely none. But she was a splendid cook, and a gracious hostess, and had it not been for the basic flaw in her character, incurable deceit, she would have been an admirable and lovable woman despite her lack of intellectual brilliancy.

Mr. Charles occasionally uses the word "calie"—the Gaelic word for a visit or friendly call. Mr. Spurr, the Baptist minister,[15] introduced this word into Cavendish. When he came over from Nova Scotia he brought it with him and it soon became quite at home in our vocabulary. "Off on a calie" or "gone cali-

---

15   Rev. Spurr was the adoptive father of LMM's childhood friend, Nate Lockhart. Nate's father, Nathan Joseph Lockhart, was a sailor who had died at sea shortly before his son was born. Nate's mother Nancy remarried a Baptist minister, John Church Spurr, who eventually adopted Nate (even so, at some point Nate began to go by his father's name, Lockhart). The correct spelling of "calie"— that is, a Scottish country dance—is ceilidh.

eing" is a common expression there to this day. Of course that is not the right way to spell it. I like the word myself. It has a pleasant, homely, friendly sound to me—perhaps because I heard it so often on the lips of old friends who sleep in Cavendish churchyard—Mr. Charles among them. It brings to mind many a delightful autumn or winter afternoon when I took my fancy work and "went on a calie" to the home of some girl friend. "Calies" were sociable things.

Mr. Chas. faithfully records all the bushels of grain sown each spring and harvested in the fall. Of course this sowing was done by the seeder then and for many years before. But I well remember the years before the "seeder" came into its own. When I was very small there were no "seeders." All the grain was sown by hand. I can recall very vividly seeing Grandfather striding across the red fields scattering seed from a particular kind of basket slung from a rope around neck and shoulder. There were people I believe who had the knack of "sowing with both hands" but I never saw any of them at work. Such gifted individuals could of course sow a field in just half the time required by the others.

One spring day Mr. Chas. "ploughed the little field." Well do I know that "little field." It was on the left hand as one entered the gate, filling up the space between the road and the barns. As the barns were slightly higher the drainage from stables and manure sheds seeped down into that field making it "rich beyond the dreams of avarice" as far as soil went. Consequently its crop was always a bumper one, grain growing there higher than a man's head. Mr. Charles indulged the peculiar whim of building his barns and all other out-buildings between his house and the main road, so that all comers had to pass along his lane through a passage formed by the barns on the left and granary, greenhouse, pighouse and "boiler house" and hen house on the right. But nobody ever seemed to mind that when the friendly eye of the little white house beyond winked genial greeting. The real drawback was that the barns to some extent spoiled what would otherwise have been a glorious unhindered view of the gulf from the doorstep of the back door. And that was a pity, nice barns as they were. Very nice and very neat. Always beautifully whitewashed with red painted doors and windows. Mr. Charles had a passion for whitewashing. Every spring he whitewashed not only his house, well-house and outbuildings, but the fence posts down the lane. Nobody else in Cavendish ever went as far as that, though most people whitewashed their houses and barns, if they were not painted. When I came to Ontario the big gray, unpainted barns gave me at first a certain impression of shiftlessness. A P.E. Islander was considered "shiftless" if his barns were neither painted nor whitewashed. And I must say I do not think Ontario's gray barns add much to the beauty of her landscape or her farmsteads.

Certainly all through his diary Mr. Charles does not impress one as a man who was at all proud of his family, whether it was a Scotchman's affected humility or not. But one of his gloomy predictions at least did not come true: "The boys are not likely to make good farmers. Too much hurry sometimes." They all turned out excellent farmers, industrious and hard working and no one would ever accuse them of being in a hurry over anything.

"Pensie gone after Jacks to shear sheep" evokes a host of quaint old memories. The sheep-shearing was an annual event on Cavendish farms and was a mixture of interest and horror to us young fry. Large flocks of sheep were kept in those days and the evening gambols of the lambs around the fields were delightful to see. The "Jack girls"—"Old Margaret" and her niece Sarah—went around sheep shearing. They arrived on the morning of the eventful day carrying their shears and their "sheep shearing" clothes in a bundle. These they promptly put on—and very dirty, greasy, unpleasant garments they were. Shearing unwashed sheep was a dirty job—and in those days the sheep were never washed before shearing. The Jack "girls" were not noted for their beauty at any time and in those shearing togs they were good understudies for Macbeth's witches.

The sheep were driven into the sheep house and a shearing table was erected. Maggie, with fatal eye, selected and seized a sheep, swung it to the table, hobbled its legs and began shearing. Clip-clip went the skilled shears. The fleece fell away, so white and clean and silvery on its under side. The sheep emerged from it, an odd bare figure, scampering away in amazement at her escape and transformation. I often wondered what a sheep thought about while she was being shorn. They generally lay very still. Was it the calm of despair? A "good" shearer never wounded the sheep. But sometimes with even the most expert the shears bit too deep and the sheep scampered away with a red stain on her flank. At the end of the day the shearers were paid at the rate of 4 cents a sheep. Not too much surely. I would not have sheared a sheep, even supposing I had been able to, for 4 dollars much less cents.

The "horror" of the day centred about the lambs. Those poor pretty frisky lambs who had never known pain. How my heart bled for them. Their tails were cut off that day. I was told it had to be and I suppose it had, though to this day I do not understand why it was necessary. Oh, those poor little bleeding lambs, running to their mothers to be comforted, bleating pitifully. The wounds seemed to heal quickly and next day the lambs would seem normal enough. But I don't think they ever scampered around the fields at sunset quite so light-heartedly again.

After the sheep shearing the wool-washing was a day's work. It was always done outside. A fire was kindled under the big potato boiler, the tubs were taken out and the wool washed and spread on the grass to dry. When dry it was bagged and carried away to the carding mill, whence it came back in those beautiful soft glossy rolls of floss. Grandma spun them on her little spinning wheel. She never used the large wheel. At Park Corner they spun in the garret. They had two large spinning wheels which are there to this day. Women like spinning. I think I would have liked it myself if I had ever had a chance to learn it. But grandma had given up spinning long before I grew up. Spinning went on at Park Corner till Aunt Annie's death. Stella and Frede were expert spinners.

Then came knitting and weaving. Very few people weave now on the Island but when I was a child many did. Amanda's mother always wove up in their garret. What a fascination it was to watch her. A great many people, however, hired "the Jacks" to do their weaving for them. As I recall it those Jacks were really very useful members of the community. They spun and wove and sheared sheep, planted and picked potatoes, bound sheaves, and plaited hats from the wheat straw. Somebody was always getting the Jacks to do something—there were three of them. "Old Jane," Old Margaret and Sarah, who was young then but is old now. Margaret died last year—nearly a hundred years old. But Jane died over twenty years ago. And they sent for me to take a picture of her in her coffin!!! It was a ghastly performance. The coffin had to be propped up almost on end before the window. The resulting picture, however, looked exactly like old Jane—who looked no weirder in her coffin than she did in life. What a craving the human heart has to keep some poor "counterfeit presentment" of its loved and lost. It is a little hard to conceive of anyone loving Jane Jack but no doubt her sister and her parents did. Old Mr. Jack died before my recollection but I remember old Mrs. Jack, who was not at all a bad-looking old lady and must have been quite comely in her youth. She was always spinning at her little wheel with a white frilled cap around her face. How odd it would be to see an old lady nowadays with a cap! Yet I do not know that our old ladies have gained so much in giving up caps. They were quite becoming to lined faces and graying hair. And the caps for state occasions were very "dressy" and becoming. I remember (Step) Grandmother Montgomery was noted for her smart caps. When she went to an evening festivity she always carried her cap in a box with her. Old "Grandma Campbell"—Frede's grandmother—and Great Aunt Ellen always wore little hood-like caps of black net with a black ruching around the face. But these were thought old-fashioned by up-to-date old ladies who perched little confections of lace and ribbon on the top of their heads and called them "caps," much to the scorn of still older dames who condemned such new-fangled vagaries and predicted dire things of the state of society which permitted them. What would they have said if they could have seen the lady I saw in church last Sunday—sixty if she was a day and her white hair bobbed. And am I in my turn as antiquated as those scornful dames of long ago when I assert that I thought she looked very pitiful and ridiculous?

The present mania for bobbed hair is becoming to young fresh faces. But I think it is very cruel to the faded and aged—and indeed to all who are past their first youth.

"Mercy me," as those ladies of the last century would have said. Where have I wandered to from Mr. Charles' sheep-pen? Let us get back to our muttons and see if "the Jacks" have finished his sheep. Yes, and been paid 88 cts. only, having shorn 22 sheep. Sweet be their slumbers.

But on that very eve it "looks like rain" and Mr. C. predicts the "sheep storm." Evidently it did not come just then but come it certainly would. The "sheep storm" never missed. It had nothing to do with the sheep but it was a June storm, invariably coming soon after the sheep were shorn. The wind would set in from the northeast, bitterly cold and blow hard from that direction for two and sometimes three days, with driving stinging rain. The unlucky sheep, their warm coats reft away, would feel it bitterly. Hence the name. I am afraid I did not sympathize properly with the poor animals for I always liked the sheep storm. There was such a bite and tang to it. I would like to see a sheep storm again. They never come in Ontario.

On Wednesday, July 13, 1898, there is a curious entry about a wedding. There is not a word in it to indicate that it was his own daughter Pensie's wedding. Mr. Charles was evidently very inarticulate when it came to the great changes of life.

I remember that I felt very sore over that wedding. Pensie and I had been intimate friends all our lives. But she never even told me she was going to be married. Everybody knew it for her dressmaker had given the secret away. Two or three days before her wedding day she came up for the mail and as usual I "went a piece" home with her. But she might have

(Step) Grandmother
Montgomery

been a hundred years away from getting married for anything she said. Two days afterward she was married, having only two or three of her cousins on the spindle side[16] in to see her.

I was deeply hurt—and the hurt remained for a long time. I think I was justified in feeling hurt. It was a strange way for Pensie to behave. But the pain has long vanished and I can make excuses for Pensie now which I was too sore to make then. She had some of her father's odd streaks in her and one of them was an inability to tell or talk of any such matter—just as the very entry in his diary about her wedding shows. I did not understand this then and I resented

---

16　That is, on the female side.

Pensie's silence for a long time. I went to see her once in her new home; but New Glasgow was seven miles away and it was not easy for me to get over. I suppose I did not try very hard, after her strange behavior. But I am glad to think that in the year before her death we met oftener and the old friendship put forth an autumnal blossom again. The old bitterness had worn itself out. The last time I saw Pensie was one winter evening. I went over and spent the whole evening with her. She was in bed but did not know her condition was so serious and hoped to recover. I knew better and under my outward gayety I felt very sad. We had one of our old evenings of chat and gossip and jokes. She died very soon afterwards. She has been dead nearly twenty years. But while I have been writing this she has been alive. I have heard her laughter, seen the flash of her blue eyes, the toss of her auburn curls. She is gone—and Mr. and Mrs. Charles have gone—and the old Cavendish has gone. But it lives again in Mr. Charles' old diary and I am loth to cease writing of it. It has been a refuge—an escape from the bitter, worried present; I hate to leave it and come back to 1925! For life now is a bitter harassed thing for me, always in bondage to a great dread; and there are times when I envy Pensie, asleep in her unmarked grave on the New Glasgow hillside. "The one shall be taken and the other left."[17]

---

17   Matthew 24:40: "Then shall two be in the field; the one shall be taken, and the other left."

Index